Main Street

Main Street

HEART of WEXFORD

NICKY ROSSITER

To my family: Anne, Mark, David, Kate, Paula, Ellie, Finn,
Lola, Ziggy, Jude, Jack and Noah

With special thanks to Mr & Mrs James O'Connor, whose
encouragement and access to research materials assisted so many of
my publications

First published 2018

The History Press
The Mill, Brimscombe Port
Stroud, Gloucestershire, GL5 2QG
www.thehistorypress.co.uk

British Library Cataloguing in Publication Data.
A catalogue record for this book is available from the British Library.

ISBN 978 0 7509 8754 7

Typesetting and origination l
Printed by TJ International l

Contents

—⁓—

Introduction

Wexford is one of the few towns or cities in Ireland, and indeed the United Kingdom, where Main Street is still the official name of the main retail and commercial street of the town. In Dublin this honour goes to O'Connell or Grafton Street. In Cork it is Patrick Street and in London Regent Street or one of a myriad of other roads. In Wexford the Main Street is the location of most of the shops and as such its length is still traversed regularly by locals and visitors. Despite this there are hidden gems of buildings and past history that are overlooked.

Our Main Street is 'topped and tailed' with two ancient settlements: at the north end is Selskar, reputed to be the Celtic origin of the town, while to the south is Stonebridge and the Viking section of Wexford. Both are generally incorporated in Main Street and therefore they are included here.

In an earlier book I looked at the streets of Wexford but avoided Main Street because it would have doubled the size of that volume.

This book will look at the development of Main Street and its division into North and South Main Street. It will trace – where possible – the development of particular premises through directories, old advertisements, historical documents and anecdotes.

Wexford's Main Street is almost 100 per cent commercial with very few public buildings located there. This was not always the case and some of the earlier uses for familiar edifices or sites may surprise even the natives.

The material included will broaden our understanding of the historical commercial growth and decline of a port town that is also the county administrative centre.

The majority of illustrations are directly from my own collection or provided by friends. If any copyright or attribution is infringed please let me know and it will be corrected in any future edition.

Background

Main Street is probably one of the oldest thoroughfares in Wexford. Unfortunately, until the 1800s it was one of the least mentioned, partly because the term and title Main Street was not in common use. This refers not just to Wexford but also to other countries where the principal streets might be called Market Street or High Street. Even in the United States, where main street exists but has a different meaning, it is believed to date only from around 1810.

We all too often forget that religion played a huge part in the lives of our ancestors well into the seventeenth century. People saw themselves as being from a parish rather than a street, even in urban environments like Wexford. The parish, in turn, gave titles to the streets and these were usually saints' names such as Ivory's (Iberius or Ibar), Bridget's, or perhaps Selskar from the abbey that dominated it. Matters are further complicated by what are seen as old maps but which were drawn more from memory and descriptions that show a street depicted as Main Street from an era when it almost certainly did not have such a designation. Likewise, history books can tell us tales of Cromwell's troops 'rampaging along Main Street from the Castle', again at a time when such a title did not apply to that street. In fact, 'rampaging into Stonebridge' would have served better.

As commerce increased we are indebted to directories such as Slater's and the magnificent Bassett's, but again while giving us some excellent information they also cause confusion in that many businesses are listed with an address as simply 'Main Street', or even when listed with a number it does not tell us what numbering system applied at the time. We do not know exactly when the designations of North and South Main Street began to be used.

There is even confusion over the building numbers because sometimes people were rather cavalier in deciding a number and then more often than not, even with reliable numbering, buildings were expanded and might incorporate two earlier buildings but use only one house number with the other lost. Even in the twenty-first century, builders, developers and owners seem to conspire against the historian. There are now two sets of premises with the addresses 98 and 100 South Main Street. One of these pairs actually disrupts the whole numbering system, bringing even numbers to the side of the street used for odd numbers.

About the Author

Nicky Rossiter, as locals say, 'was born and reared in Wexford'. He has been writing about local and social history for three decades and this will be his thirteenth full-length book on the town. He stresses that other than one such title all the material has related to the actual town of Wexford – 'inside the ring road' – and is still not an exhausted seam of heritage and history.

Nicky has been published in various newspapers, magazines and journals and broadcast locally and nationally, including a regular series on South East Radio called 'Stories'. He was the founder of Wexford Youth Theatre and wrote a number of plays for them, which were performed on stage and radio.

Nicky lives outside Wexford with his wife Anne and continues to research the town and its history.

1

History

The Viking Town

It was with the settlement of the Norsemen in this area that we would see a town begin to develop. The harbour was often the most important place in a Viking town and Wexford would not have been very different, although what later became Main Street would probably have made up much of the seafront. Here, boats were loaded and unloaded with goods and animals. Markets were held on the rudimentary quay that was very different from that of today or even two centuries ago. Nearby, boat-builders, potters, leatherworkers, carpenters and other craftspeople were busy in their workshops. The town was a self-sustaining unit with people making or trading the essentials of life. Wexford continued to grow over the next 200 years with trails developing into rudimentary streets.

Norman and Medieval Wexford

After 1169 and the coming of the Normans, Wexford developed even further as a town. The following description of a medieval town could well have described the Wexford of the period:

Outside the wall, all the town's rubbish is dumped. Pigs and dogs root around in the muck. Inside the walls there are many grand buildings such [as] the homes of the merchants, a monastery and the churches. The lanes are busy with people, especially on market day and on fair days, when people come from miles around to visit the town. They trade in cloth, in food and in other products. There are beggars, rich men and foreign traders, all mingling in the narrow lanes and on the quays. The town does not smell very nice. The butcher's shops in areas called The Shambles are the smelliest of all apart from the tannery. The tanner turns animal skins into leather keeping them in pits of animal excrement. There are signs hanging from many of the shops and they display pictures instead of words. This is because the majority of people cannot read or write. People come to recognise the pictures for the most popular shops. On the street corners are barrels full of water because most houses are wooden and the water barrels are there in case of fire.

In the medieval town daily life was very regulated with a typical timetable:

4 a.m.:   The bell rang to announce the first Mass of the day and the end of the nightwatchman's duty.
6 a.m.:   Shops and market stalls opened.
8 a.m.:   Foreign merchants were allowed to start trading.
9 a.m.:   Breakfast.
3 p.m.:   Most shops and market stalls closed.
8 p.m.:   Curfew bell. Town gates closed, houses shut up, the night watch began.

This picture shows North Main Street looking south from the Bullring. Tommy Roche's public house replaced Jack Fane's, where Tommy had worked as a barman. Hamilton's is on the right. The metal pole for carrying electricity wires was a common sight on our Main Street. (Rossiter Collection)

Looking at Wexford's Main Street today we see a vastly changed area from those Viking and medieval 'towns'. In fact, what we now call Main Street divided into North and South is made up of a number of old streets that have been subsumed and adapted into that one long commercial stretch running parallel to the harbour. If we did not divide the street it would probably rightly claim the title of the longest main street in Ireland at 0.46 Irish miles, or 0.59 statute miles. There is an old Wexford saying about the Main Street that says, 'the further it goes the meaner [pronounced mainer] it gets'. However, in true Wexford fashion the saying never states which end this starts from, so people from each end can still feel good.

Starting at the north end of what is commonly thought of as Wexford Main Street, we actually walk on Selskar Street before entering what was once Foreshore Street to take you to the Common Plain, or the Bullring as it is now called. We then proceed along Main Street North and South – together once known as Fore Street – before ending our sojourn at Stonebridge. It is difficult to ascertain when the north and south designations were added because many of the older advertisements referred simply to Main Street. This also causes problems in locating some of the older shops. The older use of Fore Street reminds us of the general geographic origin of names with Fore Street and the next street away from the seafront as Back Street, later Upper Back Street and eventually High Street. The Main Street designation probably dates from the proliferation of shops and other businesses that made it the principal or main street of Wexford. But if one looks above the shop signs you will see in many instances the original buildings from the time when they were family homes, including examples of the multi-paned 'Wexford Window'.

The topography of a town such as Wexford 1,000 or more years ago is hard to imagine by those used to its twenty-first century configuration. The first thing we must accept is that there are no shops and this in essence means that what we know as the Main Street was a very different environment. Physically Wexford was very different in those times in that the waters of the harbour covered what we now see as the quay front. Try to visualise the town without buildings and look at the physical contours of hills and depressions such as the steep decline from Main Street at Anne Street and the rise in the ground of South Main Street after Peter's Street. Features such as these remind us of the contours of the 'Celtic', Norse and Norman towns or settlements.

The traditional explanation for the existence of our long Main Street is that the original settlement of Wexford was in the Selskar area with the later Norse settlement located at the opposite end of the present street around the Bishopswater River. Interaction and trade between the two was said to result in the development of a trail that later became populated and thus evolved into Main Street. This is a very simplistic view but, like all such myths, it can have some basis in fact.

Selskar Street

This section of the street takes its title from the parish of Selskar, which in turn borrows from the Church of St Sepulchre, which we recall as Selskar Abbey. A less ecclesiastical derivation is also possible. Selskar may mean 'Seal Rock'. The Norse used the word 'skar' to refer to rocks, as in Tuskar, and the Rock of Wexford is situated just 150 yards from the abbey. Dr George Hadden, writing in the *Journal of Wexford Historical Society* and with a keen eye for land and seascape and an unrivalled knowledge of the history of Wexford town, postulated the existence of a prehistoric market located around the present Cornmarket, centuries before the arrival of the Vikings. Where Hadden had located an early Christian oratory at Selskar, Dr Billy Colfer suggests a larger, circular monastic enclosure, partly delineated by the curved street pattern in the Selskar area. A settlement would have grown around the oratory, benefiting from and supplying services to the monks.

In common with most towns, the street was primarily residential with the townhouses of the gentry mixed with the more humble dwellings of the general population in places such as Trimmer's Lane and Well Lane.

Foreshore Street

This is a self-explanatory name for the section of our present North Main Street stretching from Selskar Street (roughly at George's Street) to the Bullring. As the name suggests, the waters of the harbour once brushed the land here. It was renamed Lower Main Street in the 1700s but later became North Main Street. Buildings were erected on the western side and as the land was reclaimed for a growing population others grew up on the opposite side.

The Bullring

This area of Main Street connects to the Common Quay via Common Quay Street and, having once been noted as the Common Plain, we surmise that it was an area for fairs and markets in the days prior to the development of the modern retail shop.

The Golden Mile

This is the common designation, probably coined by estate agents – in Wexford parlance auctioneers – describing the Main Street from the Bullring to Coffey's Hill. This is, and has always been, the hub of commerce for Wexford and includes almost equal portions of North and South Main Street. It is in this area of Main Street that the eponymous description of Wexford as 'Tumbling Down' in Billy Roche's book is most striking. The houses on the seaward side usually had (and still have) cellars or lower floors covering the land sloping down towards the seafront. On the opposite sides many of the later shops had dual-height ground floors where they expanded into the yards or gardens at their rear, sloping upwards to High Street or Back (Mallin) Street.

Stonebridge

Main Street ends its stretch southward at King Street with the final portion consisting mainly of Stonebridge. It takes its name from what was a small bridge located there. It has been called Wexford Bridge and in 1764 it was known as Jew's Bridge. The bridge was built over the Bishopswater River and may have marked the northern gate of the earliest Norse or Viking settlement.

Dr Hadden visualised the Norse entering by the Bishopswater River and hauling their longships ashore just below the knoll or mound on which the present military barracks is situated. In 1987, when businessman Colman Doyle began clearing a site at the corner of Bride Street and South Main Street, some timbers were noted protruding from the ground. With the agreement of Mr Doyle the National Museum was informed and archaeologist Edward Bourke was dispatched to Wexford to excavate. Bourke later described finding the remains of 'two Viking houses and a lean-to shed. House One was of a single post and wattle construction with a floor of hardened estuarine mud. Another house had walls of sharpened planks, driven directly into the earth, with a floor similar to house One.' The walls of the lean-to building were also of plank construction, the floor was composed of sand, and the roof was probably thatched with straw or reeds. Both houses were provisionally dated to the early eleventh century. This gives us the first concrete indication of the type of houses that would have populated Main Street more than a millennium ago.

Over the following centuries Wexford grew greatly in size and importance, as evidenced by the description of the town by Giraldus Cambrensis in 1169 as 'surrounded by ramparts probably of stone'. Norse Wexford was a trading post of some significance. Giraldus tells us that the Normans tried to commandeer a ship carrying corn and wine from Bristol but were foiled in the attempt by quick-thinking sailors. The abundance of ships belonging to the Wexford Norse is attested by references in the annals to their part in the raids on Cork and Waterford and in their ability to transport numbers of troops from Wexford to Dublin in 1128. Giraldus also states that Wexford traded hides of animals for imported wine.

Dr Billy Colfer considered the Norse Wexford to be slightly larger and notes, 'There is a natural break in the street pattern where the curved line of the street at Cornmarket could well represent the line of the Norse defences', indicating the growth of Norse Wexford from that original site. This is supported by a report in Hore's *History of Wexford* that, in the eighteenth century, the remains of the Norse wall could be seen at Common Quay. Colfer continues, 'If, as seems probable, the Norse town ended at Cornmarket, it would have consisted of four intramural parishes with a combined area of about twenty-five acres. This point is substantiated by the fact that market places were typically situated to the south-east or east of monastic enclosures and Cornmarket is about 200m directly south-east of Selskar Abbey.

The area just outside the Norse town – the present Bullring – may have been held in common by both 'sides' and may be why even centuries later in 1621 it was referred to as the Common Plain. Further development would ensue with the arrival of Norman forces in 1169, including the extension of the town to take in the older settled area around Selskar. But this was a very different street to what we see today. The buildings would have been well scattered with gardens and animal pens to provide food for the households. Buildings would have been single storey and only over a long period of time would construction develop from wattle and daub through timber to stone-built houses. Even in London it took until the late 1600s for most buildings to be constructed of stone.

Throughout this and for most of its later history we must bear in mind that Main Street was residential, as were all towns of an era prior to 'ready money' and generally manufactured goods. During that time most goods that could not be made at home or by neighbours were purchased in a few very small shops attached to manufactories, such as those producing gloves, hose and hats in areas such as Cornmarket or on the quay. Otherwise people used the fairs or markets or bought from travelling peddlers.

In the Middle Ages there were few permanent shops but every town had a market. Often if you wanted to buy or sell anything you went to the local market or waited for the regular fairs. Medieval shops were really workshops where the customer could walk in; there were no glass windows. In towns in the Middle Ages there were craftsmen such as carpenters, bakers, butchers, blacksmiths, bronze smiths, fletchers (arrow makers), bowyers (bow makers), potters, coopers, and barber surgeons who both cut hair and pulled teeth. The number of shops grew in the seventeenth century. Meanwhile, glass became much cheaper and in the eighteenth century shops began to have glass windows. By the eighteenth century there were many small shops in every town, including shoemakers, drapers, milliners, haberdashers, bakers, butchers, grocers, fishmongers, booksellers and gunsmiths.

As stated in the article 'Consumption and Living Conditions 1750–2016', drawings of Dublin in the mid-eighteenth century showed street traders hawking an array of goods from coarse earthenware to turf and foodstuffs for 'households of the middling and lower orders'. It also notes that the communications revolution from the 1840s facilitated retailing expansion: 'Small shops proliferated in smaller towns selling dry goods, food, drink, hardware and household goods.' It was in the mid- to late nineteenth century that the larger shops such as Musgrave's in Cork and Clery's in Dublin were set up. Wexford would have followed a similar timeline in the establishment of its retail concentration on Main Street.

Looking at the buildings that now populate Main Street, we note that most date to the early 1800s, which was a major period of expansion in the town with the construction of the linear quay front replacing the many wharves and jetties that often later became lanes leading from Main Street. Even one of our older buildings, the famous Kenny's Hall where Cromwell is said to have resided in 1649, is recorded as 'reputedly incorporating fabric of earlier seven-bay two-storey timber-frame house, *c.*1600'. Prior to that it is most likely that the houses were lower as residences. With retailing growing there was a tendency to build upwards with the ground floor as a retail outlet and two floors of living quarters above, giving the more familiar three-storey house of Main Street.

Up until these major developments there was little need for a major drainage system. Toilets were drained into cesspits and 'clean' waste water would have been tossed into the 'open drain' that ran along the centre of the road or street. With increased traffic, and as the street became commercialised, this drain was covered with flat slabs making 'box drains'. It was only with the introduction of piped water that more sophisticated drainage systems had to be installed.

Finding the first mention of a Main Street proves difficult, but as we look back through various directories we find the following:

1764 – Flesh Market; Cornmarket; Back Street; Shambles; Keizars [*sic*] Lane; Ferryboat Quay; Medows [*sic*] Quay; Bennett's Quay; Common Quay; Gibson's Lane; Custom House Quay (principal quay). (Griffith's Valuation)

The first mention is in 1820 in *Pigot's Directory*:

1820 – Back; *Main*; Selskar; John; Cornmarket; Slaney; Westgate; Old Pound; Common Quay; Faith; Custom House Quay; Bullring; Castle; Monck; Anne; Mary; Ram; Paul Quay; Stonebridge; George.

The *Dublin Almanac* of 1844 gives us the first description of the street:

Quay c. 800 yards from bridge to just above barracks. Another parallel 1000 yards long, narrow, about 130 yards from quay. Another Street was c. 220 yards from quay. Lanes were connecting. 'Airy district 450 × 130 winging west side of town's middle part. Straggling airy Street extends 500 yards NW along Taghmon/New Ross road to obelisk near windmills. Another road goes 250 yards NE to new gaol. Bullring, Courthouse, Parish Church, diverging streets to Back Street & Selskar, Johns Lane/Chapel Lane to John Street.'

The oldest building in any town is difficult to ascertain, and indeed this might not have been on Main Street. In Wexford one of the first buildings to be identified is what we often called Kenny's Hall, which stood on the site now occupied by Penney's. Although much altered over the centuries, it was the residence of Colonel David Stafford in 1649. It later passed through a number of owners and these will be considered in a later section. We are aware of the building and date because of the legend that Oliver Cromwell spent some time there.

Hore's *History of Wexford* states: 'Nearly all the houses in the Main Street … were the residences of better class people in the past, the business portion of the town being Cornmarket and Back Street.' The landed gentry had townhouses in which they spent most of the winter and entertained their friends at other periods such as Assize Week in spring and summer.

The Nunn family had townhouses in both north and south Main Street, later occupied by Rossiter's ironmongery and Keegans respectively. Harveys of Killiane had their town residence in what later became the Imperial Hotel on Selskar Street. Hore states, 'The old Norman family of Herron resided in the eighteenth century in the large house on South Main Street now occupied by the constabulary.' Colonel Tottenham lived 'in a spacious house' near the Bullring that was later occupied by Godkins. Miss Kitty Ford of Ballyfad House lived for many years in another house near the Bullring that later became Mernagh's confectionery shop. Leigh's of Rosegarland also had their town house facing the Bullring. Archdeacon Elgee – father of 'Speranza', the mother of Oscar Wilde – occupied the rectory on Main Street that was later Messrs Wheelock's. Esmonde's town house was further south, almost facing Anne Street, and part of it was used as a booking office for the coach service to Dublin.

Again from Hore writing in 1906 we learn, 'about eighty or ninety years ago there were no shops in the Main Street then called Fore Street. All the houses were residences of landowners and persons of independent means. All that class has disappeared from Wexford within the last sixty years and their residences have been converted into shops.'

Even then Main Street retained a very high number of permanent residents, as we see in a casual glance at the census of 1911.

At number 2 we had the Richards family, consisting of mother, father, two grown children and a servant. Meanwhile, number 11 gives us a picture of a business with 'live-in staff' connected to the retail shop. There were the Byrne family of five as well as four young adult males designated 'boarder draper assistant' and two female servants. At number 3 there was a family of two adults with four young children and the sister-in-law of the 'head of house'. Finally, the Wheelock family at number 4 North Main Street had a household on census night of the head of the house, his brother and sister, three boarders and a servant, as well as a 'visitor'.

A large number of the houses on the east side would have been owned or rented by people associated with the growing marine trade of the harbour. These often had jetties connecting the rear of the house to the seafront in order to access cargoes and boats. There is evidence in pictures of some of these homes dating from the late twentieth century of doors on a level of what must have been later cellars accessing a former shorefront many feet below the level of Main Street.

Shops then opened on ground floor areas, but it was not always a street of commerce and retail. Wexford Main Street has been home to churches, cinemas, hotels, newspaper offices and printing works, undertakers, a mechanics' institute, trade union offices, a jail, corporation chambers, a courthouse, and reputedly a public house about every few doors along. An interesting quote in Jim Jenkins's book *Retailing in Wexford* is that 'one yard of counter is equal to 100 acres of land', and this no doubt became more true as the consumer society grew in Wexford and elsewhere.

The TV Service Centre was located on North Main Street. It was a common service on offer on Main Street between the days of people renting their televisions – with service included – to the more reliable, seldom-repaired flat screens of today. The shop retained a lot of the earlier features of Main Street shops such as the heavy door and the divided display window. Note also the tiling under the window and the old-style step at the entrance. Barely visible above the shop is a fairly typical window of the late nineteenth century. This had been a public house prior to the service business opening there. (Rossiter Collection)

2

Places and Events

—ɯ—

In this chapter we look closely at the buildings, shops and events that make up Wexford Main Street. Unfortunately, as with all history, there are some well-documented buildings and some that defy all our best research. Therefore we cannot give a comprehensive history for all of the 250-odd buildings on the street in question. We will include the big and the small to give a wide picture of how the town has developed through time. Where possible we will include the current building number but these are sometimes difficult due to idiosyncrasies in denoting them at different times. Buildings were amalgamated or divided, or the owners sometimes allocated a new number.

Bag Factory
It is hard to believe that there was once a bag factory on South Main Street. This was for the production of paper bags not handbags and was part of Harahan's, who were also printers, wholesale stationers and paper merchants at 14 South Main Street. The factory was upstairs from the shop with a printing works to the rear extending up to High Street. The bag factory employed a dozen girls making bags of all sizes for the grocery trade. The printing works had its own electricity supply that was shared with the Theatre Royal next door. When the theatre was in use printing ceased. It is said that the works had a ghost – possibly the same as the one at the theatre – Johnny Hoey.

Banks
Most of the banks in Wexford were established on the quays. This was natural in that they were 'following the money', with maritime trade and fisheries the prime earners well into the twentieth century.

Between 1770 and 1780, Walter and Thomas Redmond founded Redmond's Bank and it was flourishing in 1785. Walter later retired and Thomas continued until the business was vested in John Redmond, who also had a bank in Enniscorthy. By 1823 the registered partners in Redmond's Bank were John Brennan, Michael Devereux and John and Richard Redmond of Rocklands. Redmond's Bank was in the Bullring in a house later occupied by grocer James Kelly. In 1811 Archibald and Isaac Wood, who lived next door, robbed it. They are said to have hidden the proceeds in a large kettle that acted as a sign over their shop. However, they were discovered and Archibald was sentenced to be burned on the hand and to be transported for seven years. Isaac was acquitted. When this bank failed in 1834 all creditors were paid and business was transferred to the new local branch of the Bank of Ireland, with John E. Redmond as manager. On a map dated 1840 this bank was located on Main Street (opposite Anne Street) in premises later occupied by Joyce's Hardware.

Wexford Savings Bank took out a large notice in the *Independent* in 1858 that included a note of its assets (deposits) of £18,021 11*s* 9*d* from 613 depositors, as well as two charitable bodies and four friendly societies. The following year the assets were noted as £16,675 10*s*, with individual depositors reduced to 566 while retaining the other bodies.

Beechville Dairy

Not many people in Wexford will remember this but in 1947 it was the official name of Jack Pettit's shop at the top of Oyster Lane. In those days he not only sold milk but delivered 130 gallons per day. He had started work early on each of those days because as well as delivering he had to collect the milk from local farms.

Birmingham and Sheffield Warehouse

This is another interesting outlet advertised in 1845 but with only Main Street given as an address. The proprietors were listed as Stafford and Carroll. It appears to have been an existing business as they refer to enlarging both stock and premises in their appeal to 'The Nobility, Gentry and Public in general'. Among the stock on offer one could find British Plate Ware 'all warranted'; 'cuttlery' [*sic*] of every description; coal vases, plate buckets; shower and hip baths; and table and chamber candlesticks. They offered, 'hoop, sheet, rod and bar iron' as well as 'cast, blister, shear and spring steel'. Not wasting any advertising money, they had a P.S.: 'A respectable Lad will be taken as an apprentice' and 'Furnished Lodgings to be Let'.

Book Centre

It first opened it Wexford beside the current Hasset's in what was earlier Fortes Café, which was renowned for its chips and sausage teatime treat on a Saturday for those working in retail when the shops stayed open until 7.30p.m. Dessert was an 'orange soda' – a dollop of ice cream in a glass of orange Crush. Frank Hall, of Radio Telefís Eireann, officially opened the Book Centre in Wexford on 13 June 1975. The first celebrity author was Eilis Dillon, who appeared there on 16 June of that year. The shop later moved to 5 South Main Street.

Bookie Offices

This was the local term for the turf accountants. I recently learned that off-course betting in such establishments only became legal in the United Kingdom in the early 1960s; in Wexford they were a feature of our landscape for decades before that. These were a far cry from the modern betting office of plush chairs, coffee machines and live TV broadcasts; back then most were about the size of a generous 'front room' and probably started out as such. There was a counter, a glassed-off section where the 'computing staff' sat and the racing pages of the daily newspapers pinned around the walls. The 'dockets' were a mainstay of the local printing offices, with the blue carbon paper giving the punter or 'backer' a copy. Many avid gamblers on the horses were housewives and they usually kept a supply of pads of dockets at home. Betting was only on horses at the time and there was no 'hanging about' in the betting shops as there is now; many people placed the bets then went off shopping before returning home to tune in for 'the results' on BBC Radio after *Mrs Dale's Diary* that evening. Having the dockets at home often meant 'the young lad' bringing down the bet. In such case he – very seldom was it left to girls – either asked an adult to bring it in or else dashed in, placed it on the counter and ran outside to wait the call to come in to get the 'receipt' after it was time-stamped on the little machine on the counter.

It is difficult to recall the number of betting offices on Main Street in those days before the multinationals but we had Cullimores, Corcoran's, Cadogan's, and Codds (Louis and later Nancy) among others.

Boston House

This was the international sounding title of a shop opened on the corner of South Main Street and Allen Street by Mrs D. Mullett, who advertised herself as 'late Birmingham, Boston and Kolwak [*sic*]'. It offered hardware and fancy goods with 'quality high – prices low' and 'everything marked in plain figures'. She also advised readers to see the sixpence halfpenny department in Sráid Ailín (Allen Street) using her bit of the Irish language to encourage patriotic business.

Bullring

The Bullring brings us more questions than answers. It is a pivotal part of what we call Main Street but is also seen as a separate entity. First, let us look at the name. The accepted history is that the 'square' of sorts takes its name from the old sport of bull baiting, but looking critically at this one must wonder. The sport of bull baiting was certainly practised there as it was in most other British and European cities and towns. However, in most of those places, including London near Shakespeare's Globe Theatre, this was a weekly or even daily event. In Wexford it took place as a ritual based on a charter granted to the butchers of the town in 1609. The bull baiting occurred here between 1621 and 1770. Under this charter the butchers undertook to provide twice each year, on 24 August and 21 November, 'a bull to be baited by dogs'. Butchers originally supplied the bulls under this charter but this would change later. This spectacle of a huge beast tethered and then attacked by dogs originally took place at the Bullring and the hide of the animal was presented to the mayor, with the flesh being distributed to the poor of the town. Looking at the space today, one wonders how many people would have been able to attend and with only two events a year, with just a single bull each time, would the area have deserved the name? After 1800, parliamentary candidates donated the beasts and the sport was transferred to John Street, near George Street junction. The transfer probably coincided with the commercialisation of Main Street.

For many this is accepted as the site of the alleged Cromwellian massacre of 1649 in which 2,000 people were said to have died 'at the Market Cross'. Such a large number would be a major part of the population of a town such as Wexford in that era, when the population of London was just 600,000.

Another indication that the period between the late 1700s and early 1800s was the time when Main Street was developed comes from the fact that between 1770 and 1780 Redmond's Bank was founded by Walter and Thomas Redmond and it was flourishing in 1785.

In 1764 there was a courthouse with a public clock, which was a common item in an era before the general public used pocket watches or even domestic clocks. The courthouse remained until 1805. The Bullring was again called Common Plain and later Fountain Square from about 1790 to 1800, indicating that the bull baiting was no longer situated there. In 1833 it was stated to be unlit and unpaved. In 1831 Ambrose Fortune, near Bullring, advertised manufactured razors, penknives, etc., of the highest standard, and also a clock and watch business in the *Wexford Independent*.

Wexford Corporation purchased 60ft of a former shambles or meat market from Mr Sparrow for the building of the Tholsel with five arches in the early 1800s. The Court of Conscience for debts under 40s and corporation offices were at the Tholsel in 1837, with the butter market underneath. The mayor had been 'empowered to grant a lease to government of such part of the building annexed the Court of Conscience as may be necessary for a Guard Room and lock up place for prisoners'. At the turn of the nineteenth century, 'onion women' sat on the Tholsel steps twining onions; there was also a one-man Paddy's market on Common Quay, and pavement selling of second-hand clothes at the Tholsel. The Fish Market was once reputed to be called the 'Piaze' (presumably a corruption of piazza) because Wexford sailors were said to be more familiar with the Mediterranean than with Dublin. The Tholsel was demolished in 1898 and Flemish-style 'mock gable ends' were constructed to 'beautify' the area. Many people who see old photographs of the wall think it was part of the Tholsel. This gabled area was demolished in 1926.

The New Market on the seaward side of the Bullring was built in 1871, with the north side buildings replacing six thatched houses. The Corporation had been allowed to borrow £1,000 to erect this market, with the land leased from the Earl of Granard. A fire engine house was built in 1880.

In 1881 Laurence Murphy sold stationery next to Daly's Bakery, which was on the corner of the Bullring and North Main Street. Fortune & Murphy were selling 'New Masses and Offices to clergy' in the Bullring at the same time. The rectory of Archdeacon Elgee, grandfather of 'Speranza', the mother of Oscar Wilde, was in the north-east corner. This was later Pitts Coaching Inn and then Morris' Hotel and Lamberts before becoming the Diana Donnelly shop of today.

Sheppard's statue of 'The Pikeman' recalls the rebellion of 1798 when the first Irish republic was declared on this site. The Pikeman was unveiled on Sunday, 6 August 1905 by Fr Kavanagh OFM. Eleven special trains brought crowds to the event from throughout Ireland and more than twenty bands were in attendance.

Kavanagh's in the Bullring was the first garage in Wexford. It opened on 14 December 1914, selling 'Pratt's Perfection Spirit' petrol in 2 gallon cans at 2 shillings and 4 pence each. The system then was to carry these cans on the running board of the car until the engine ran low on fuel. The first Wexford petrol pump was erected here in 1919.

The Bullring has been a venue for rallies of every hue in the past few centuries, including P.T. Daly addressing a crowd on 3 August 1911 to say that dockers had won their claim and that factory workers were now urged to unionise. There was also a suffragette meeting in April 1914. There was a recruiting campaign in June 1915 by a band of the Royal Dublin Fusiliers, with pictures of the war in Belgium being projected on to the side of a van. An anti-vaccination protest was held here in 1919 and a civic commemoration of the Cromwell massacre was staged on Tuesday, 11 October 1949.

There were two air-raid shelters on the site in 1941 and an old milestone was defaced as a wartime precaution to mislead any invader, although its '64 was in Irish miles to Dublin' might have been confusing enough. The plaque to Jem Roche was unveiled on 1 October 1961. Roche is probably best known for his unsuccessful challenge for the world heavyweight boxing title against T. Burns in Dublin on St Patrick's Day in 1908. In a career of thirty-eight fights he won twenty-two by knockouts and seven on points. One of those he knocked out was John L. Sullivan. His many friends and admirers erected the plaque.

In more recent years the Bullring has hosted a variety of political rallies and celebrations of sporting victory. Before the commemoration of the 1798 rebellion there was parking around the statute. A well-known 'Del Boy' clone sold all sorts of goods from his stall each Saturday afternoon to the delight of the locals with his banter of, 'it's the change that kills me', or 'not five pounds, not even three pounds but two, yes two, for two pounds'. Many people also bought 'day-old chicks' in the Bullring with visions of self-sufficiency in the 1960s.

Businessmen for Inquests

At the turn of the century, businessmen were often called to be jury members. An illustration of this is the Ardcavan tragedy of 14 September 1900, when seven people who were going to the horse racing on the North Slob lost their lives when the boat in which they were travelling sank in Wexford Harbour.

The jury members were: John Fitzsimons, Main Street, Wexford (foreman); Matthew O'Connor, Main Street; Aid. N.J. Cosgrave, Selskar; Michael Nolan, Main Street; James Sinnott, Thomas H. Richards, Bull Ring; R.H. Shaw, Main Street; Richard Young, Main Street; John Doyle, Captain Patrick Kelly, Main Street; John P. Rochford, Main Street; James Stafford, Main Street; Michael Kelly, Monck Street; James O'Leary, Main Street, and George Daly, Bull Ring.

Cape (The)

This bar is officially called The Cape of Good Hope, a reminder of Wexford's nautical past. It was the home of the '13 club', where prospective members were required to consume thirteen glasses of punch in quick succession. A Cape Club was formed in September 1834, composed of 'government officials and upper class shopkeepers'.

Lord Kingsborough was held prisoner in the premises in 1798. In 1939 Stanley Hayes of the Bullring was prosecuted for having people on the premises at 9.50 p.m. on a Saturday night. Guard Traynor found the men in The Cape snug. Mr Hayes stated in court that he had trouble getting them to leave, and said he and his assistant already had their coats and hats on. The publican got off but the drinkers were fined 2s each.

Owen Kehoe of Selskar appeared in court for having four men drinking at 12.50 p.m. on a Sunday; he said he had agreed to let them in on his return from Mass. The publican pleaded that it was a wet day and the men had called to see if he was going to a match. The charges under the Sheebeen Act were adjourned.

Capitol Cinema

This began as a furniture store of the Stafford group and opened as a cinema on Sunday, 15 February. The opening film was *The Big Trail*, and before all the current simultaneous releases the Capitol was the second place in Ireland to show it. The cinema was advertised as 'with perfect sound'. Jack Doyle, boxer turned celebrity, and Movita Castaneda, the film actress who played exotic women/singers in films such as *Flying Down to Rio* (1933) and *Mutiny on the Bounty* (1935), made appearances in 1944 in what was billed as 'The musical extravaganza The Hit Parade' supported by Bobby Murphy's Famous

Orchestra, Cecil Hyde, 'Ireland's sensational comedian', and Scottie, 'man of a hundred instruments'. Movita later married Marlon Brando. The popularity of cinema-going at the Capitol and other venues is clear from a Corporation report in 1944 of a letter from Richard Corish (Hon. Sec. Irish Labour Party) that stated: 'Even though there are performances every night the cinemas are still overcrowded with people standing in the passages.' Eamon Doyle reminded me recently that while queuing for the latest Hopalong Cassidy film a young lad might 'make a banjo talk outside the Capitol'. That young man was Pecker Dunne.

Christmas on Main Street

Back in those dim and distant ancient days – all of fifty years ago – our first inkling of Christmas came from George Bridges. I cannot remember at what time of year

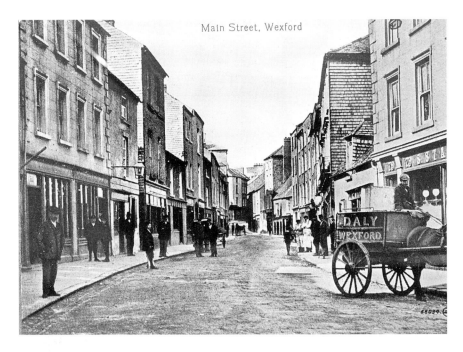

Main Street, Wexford

This old postcard shows South Main Street from the corner of Bride Street (Coffin Corner) looking north and is worth close examination. Taking a view from left to right, we suspect that the pole visible at the left-hand side may be that of North's Barber Shop, which was located there. The rather sparse street lighting indicates that this is pre-electrification of Main Street and the lantern visible above the youth is a gas light. One will notice the unpaved road and the cobble sewers (called shores in Wexford) at the side. The horse-drawn cart is delivering bread from Daly's in the Bullring and the licensed premises beside it are those of Syl Stamp. Of particular note are the gable ends visible on the buildings. These are slated rather than plastered and much of these slates came from South Wales, often as ballast in returning ships.

he started his adverts tucked into the local notes of the papers but it seems as if 'only 20 weeks to Christmas' might have been possible. If it was it gives the lie to all the present moans about Christmas advertising starting in September. Mind you, we needed the countdown back in those days when money was less available than today and credit was not a general option.

Back in those dim and distant days there seemed to be many more toy shops – rather than vast emporiums. Mr Bridges was Wexford's Santa with his little shop in Selskar being supplemented by opening the storeroom as Christmas approached. He also had a bigger shop closer to the Bullring.

However, he did not have a monopoly on our pennies. Woolworth's was the biggie back in those days – it originated as a 'five and dime' in the USA, which roughly translated to 'sixpence and a shilling' here. It was a natural magnet with a vast array of goods, but we still liked local. Next door was Woolheads and just off Main Street past King Street, Maggie Kelly was grabbing the attention of south-enders. Alfie Cadogan had a few toys and some great tricycles for the Christmas trade. O'Brien's in Selskar, a furniture shop for most of the year, even had Santa Claus in residence in December, as did Jenkins, our very own department store. At these locations you could meet the man himself and for a few bob he would give you a 'parcel'. These were gender-differentiated with pink or blue tissue paper wrapped around newspaper. Inside you would discover plastic guns, dolls and any hundreds of 'made in Hong Kong' goodies – why all the modern fuss about 'made in China'? Things were far from politically correct in those days; guns were a huge seller for the boys with everything from little tin cap guns through to cowboy sets of gun and holster to plastic machine guns that fired little grey plastic bullets – when they worked. Presents for older people included Old Spice aftershave, eau de toilette, a pair of socks or a box of chocolates.

Clay Pipes

The factory was originally on South Main Street, almost opposite Bride Street. William Murphy owned it and he later bought Miss Browne's factory at the King Street end of Barrack Street around 1889. The clay pipe was an essential in the traditional Irish wake along with the 'keeners', the 'laying out' and the tradition of stopping all clocks and covering mirrors. The family would, where possible, 'lay in' a barrel of porter, a gallon of whiskey, bread, jam, cold meats, snuff and candles, and also 'a couple of gross of clay pipes with twist tobacco'. The pipes were smoked by both genders and it is said they were steeped in porter or whiskey before use to give a 'special flavour to the tobacco'. In the late nineteenth century the pipes cost about a half penny each. The Wexford pipes were popular until wooden pipes became cheaper.

Coffey's

This department store was immortalised in a tune called 'Coffey's Hill' by the 'boys band', or to give them their proper title St Patrick's Fife and Drum Band. This may have been a reference to the marching band encountering the short steep hill in front of the shop. For many Wexford people Coffey's was probably best known for the 'approbation system'. This was a method of selling clothes and other goods when some people were either too busy or too shy to visit the shop. Getting a new jacket or pair of shoes meant that someone, usually the wife and mother, visited the shop to pick a number of possibilities. The messenger 'boy' on his distinctive bike with advertising plate and huge basket holder then delivered these to the home. The desired item was chosen in the comfort and privacy of the house – with everyone contributing a comment – and the rest were returned via the messenger. The majority of the items were then paid for 'on the book' by weekly payments. There would be queues of people paying accounts, especially on Saturday mornings as most workers were paid in cash every Friday evening. We only ever realised that approbation was a word when the sales were on and big signs went up that read 'No approbation or credit during the sale'.

This premises was the Hat and Cap Warehouse in 1877, and in 1881 as H.H. Martin's Glasgow House it advertised 'No Sloppy Goods Kept'. But by 1939 it was advertising 'An extensive yard with front on South Main Street and extending 175 feet back to open on to St Patrick's Square, opposite Henrietta Street. For sale by H.J. Coffey'.

Coffin Corner

This is located where Bride Street joins South Main Street. It was known as Coffin Corner in 1812. This may have come about from funerals from the military barracks that proceed around this corner into Bride Street heading for St Mary's graveyard. In later years, long past the designation, funeral 'removals' to Bride Street Church would take this turn, especially with removals from the County Hospital. Similarly, funerals from Bride Street Church would have come down Bride Street on to South Main Street heading for Crosstown.

Colman Doyle

The late businessman started out with his little hardware shop where once stood Stephen Doyle's and earlier Sinnott's Bacon Shop. There the by-word was, 'If we haven't got it, we will get it for you.'

Confectioners' Premises to Let

Although we have failed to locate this premises advertised to be let in 1848, we find the description to be very informative and useful in giving the reader an idea of the extent of the premises on Main Street. It was said to have been formerly occupied by Andrew Whitty, confectioner, and was being let by Mrs Hughes of Lower George's Street. The description was: 'It consists of a shop and saloon, three drawing rooms, ten bedrooms, kitchens, pantries, coal holes and bake house with good oven and large hot hearth.' It was said to be 'well worth the attentions of confectioners and fancy bakers'.

Corish Memorial Hall

This building is no longer with us. It was named to honour Richard (Dick) Corish, who was elected mayor of Wexford for twenty-five consecutive years and a member of Dail Eireann (Irish Parliament) until his death in 1945. In this building a school was started under the Agricultural and Technical Scheme. This school developed into the Vocational School and was transferred to West Gate in 1908. The Corish Memorial Hall was the Wexford headquarters of the Irish Transport and General Workers Union and also provided facilities for other clubs and organisations. The clubrooms of the Irish National Foresters Association were part of the premises but were accessed via Church Lane. The rooms always attracted the snooker and billiards enthusiasts of the town. In former days the prowess of the association's handball players was second to none.

Corry's

Corry's was, until the end of the 1900s, one of the oldest shops in Wexford, in the sense of being owned by the same family and continuing in the same business. It dated from the beginning of the nineteenth century, with the original house dating to 1825. The premises had storage stretched up to Back Street. The renovation that resulted in the new shopfront and tiling was undertaken about 1900. It traded in the past as the Manchester and Scotch House. The shop was very popular with people from rural areas who bought their haberdashery and bed linens there.

Cunningham's Boot & Shoe Warehouse

No house number was given for this but the address is rather interesting: 'South Main Street, Red House (next Gibson's Lane) and opposite Lambert's Lane – please note the address'. The lane opposite Gibson's has been Harpur's Lane in recent times and therefore must have only changed since this business was advertised in June 1871. He noted having the largest stock in Wexford and as he had a workshop 'attached to establishment' he could offer speedy repairs with the tag 'Failures in workmanship repaired free of charge'.

Dancing

In 1809 Mrs Montague advertised to teach 'that polite language, French'. Applications were to be made to her house at Selskar, 'next door but one to Mr Richards, Attorney'. Mr Montague, meanwhile, offered 'to engage to perfect grown up ladies and gentlemen in dancing in 32 teachings on payment of 1 guinea entry and 1 guinea for every 8 lessons'.

In the *Independent* in 1858 Mr T.J. DuLang advertised himself as a 'professor of dancing and kalesthenic [*sic*] exercises'. Classes could be booked at Mr Harper's in the Bullring. In 1859 the new organ at The Church of The Assumption was unveiled and the choir was conducted by Mr DuLang, with Mrs DuLang as music director. Admission on the day ranged from one shilling to one penny, but to be allowed in the sanctuary section one paid two shillings.

Dental Surgery, 1871
Mr Adolphe Davis, surgical and mechanical dentist, with a surgery at North Main Street (next door to White's Hotel) advertised that he had received Barth's Patent Apparatus for the inhalation of protoxide of nitrogen, or laughing gas, 'for painless tooth and stump extraction'.

Dental Surgery, 1914
J.D. Quinn at 73 North Main Street advertised 'gold medal artificial teeth, guaranteed comfort, durability and natural appearance'. The surgery offered 'teeth extracted by new process without pain or after effects for 1/6'. Fillings cost 2/6.

Divan (The)
Just up from the Bullring, between Jack Fane's and Mernagh's Restaurant, we had the Empire Cigar Divan. Today we only associate this name with a type of bed and many dictionaries will refer to it as an assembly of government. About a century ago the definitions included 'a coffee and smoking saloon'. While not offered as a saloon, this small shop was THE place to purchase cigars, cigarettes, pipes and tobacco.

Dun Mhuire
Hore, in his *History of Wexford*, noted that in the eighteenth century the Norman family of Heron resided here. It next came into prominence as the residence of Richard Devereux, the renowned ship-owner, whose ninety-nine schooners traded to the Baltic, the Mediterranean, Africa and Canada. He shrewdly refrained from adding one more to his fleet, lest he would become liable for a heavy income tax towards the support of the British Navy.

After the death of Richard Devereux the house became a presbytery and here the priests attached to the Church of the Assumption, Bride Street, resided from 1883 to 1889, when they transferred to the present residence in School Street. From a presbytery it became a barracks for the Royal Irish Constabulary. It was from here they kept 'law and order' in the south end of the town up to the year of their departure in 1922. During the War of Independence many a suspected 'rebel' was brought in here.

On the changeover of government the Garda Siochana were the new tenants, and it was their headquarters for some years. After their departure it was unoccupied until September 1938, when the second newly formed Praesidium of the Legion of Mary was given permission to take over the house as headquarters for their work. With the idea of erecting a much-needed hall for the parish they had the 'half unroofed buildings in the yard at the rear demolished', but the space made available was too small to warrant any building programme. A few years later, Messrs Stafford had the row of adjoining houses on their property demolished. They also purchased and 'took down' another house in the same row and had the whole site cleared before adding on another small corner section to allow a sufficient area to include a full-sized stage. They then presented all the ground to the Legion of Mary for the erection of a suitable parish hall.

The blessing of the site took place on the Feast of the Immaculate Conception, 8 December 1955, when it was decided that the hall would be named Dun Mhuire, thought to be a very suitable name indeed for a place 'that had been for so many years a semi-military Dun or Fortress, and for a Parish that is already dedicated to the Blessed Virgin Mary'. The Legion of Mary handed the site over to a parish committee to manage the hall in the best interests of the community.

In 1960, Dun Mhuire opened for concerts, dances and other entertainment. It opened on 4 December with a concert by the Artane Boys Band, with admission 2/6 to 10s. The first dance cost 6s with music by Maurice Mulcahy and his fifteen-piece orchestra. Other offerings that year included 'Musical Memories', a concert presented by the parish choir conducted by Miss M. Codd LLCM, and the Yuletide Dance, which would become an annual event similar to the Debutante Ball of Coming Out for the gentry. On 18 December they had the Opening Ceilidhe, which was a 'two-band session' featuring the local Slaneyside Ceilidhe Band and the wonderfully named Sean Donoghue & his Five Sisters from Galway.

An advertisement for Dun Mhuire in 1961 is interesting to recall:

For six nights, direct from The Olympia in Dublin Sim Sala Bim with Mandrake master illusionist – Visit a Séance – See Princess Karnac float in mid-air – Gasp as a woman is sawn in half – Meet Elastic Lady. Mas Kar the only white yogi in the world will drive a car blindfolded from Dun Mhuire to Common Quay via King Street.

The debt on the hall was reduced from £50,000 to £11,700 by 1966.

Many will recall:

Once again it is by looking above the current shops that we can understand the old Main Street. These pictures show the chimney pots of what was once the Temperance Hotel. In the days before central heating, gas and electricity most rooms had their own open fireplace. While this building was somewhat exceptional in having so many rooms one can see many of the three- and even two-storey buildings with six or seven chimney pots to this day, although most sprout weeds through lack of use. (Rossiter Collection)

When you finally reached the age of 18 years, you were old enough at last to go to the Yuletide Dance in the Parish Hall. This was the big one, the night when you would be dancing with girls for the first time. Well, you went with that intention, but some of us hadn't the courage to even look in the general direction of the girls, let alone dance with them. I knew a couple of lads who spent a lot of money getting dressed up for the big event but spent the night sitting up in the balcony too terrified to come down! Even if you did get up to dance, the local priest made sure you didn't dance too close – this was against the rules. A 'few bottles' for false courage was also out of the question. If the doorman got a whiff of alcohol off you he would send you packing. 'Neat dress essential' was on the posters and neat dress it meant – no jeans or runners, and you had to wear a tie. Unlike the Town Hall, it was impossible to 'feck in', so you had to save for a couple of weeks for the admission and to get some new gear on the 'never' in Coffey's or Johnnie Hore's.

After a lot of pressure from local musicians, the hall committee decided to hire local showbands for this annual dance. What started off with one band each year soon became a two-band session, with music being supplied mostly by The Visitors and The Supreme Seven (later Showband). Paddy Donohoe was MC for years and also pulled the tickets in the Annual Monster Draw. All proceeds from the night went to the Holy Family Confraternity Band. 'No drink, no bouncers, no drugs, and definitely no close dancing!' How on earth did we enjoy ourselves?

Dungeon (The)

The Dungeon Theatre Club opened in 1965 in a cellar under Ted Doyle's offices on North Main Street. It later became known by the less picturesque name Playhouse.

Estates

In the 1900s we in Wexford were very used to people referring to such things as the Hatton Estate, McKnight Estate or Wygram Estate. It appears that this often referred to a leasehold or ground rent on buildings that had been constructed on land owned by others such as the aforementioned families. There are maps showing much of Main Street and side streets as part of one of these estates. Such land holdings could date back to times of settlement, such as after the Cromwellian attack.

First Mayor

The first mayor of Wexford was elected in September 1840. He was Shepard Jeffares, who was in business with his brother at 30 North Main Street.

Fishers Chipper

We once had a chip shop with the very appropriate name Fishers on South Main Street. While the shop was owned and operated by the Italian Fusciardi family, it had this very local-sounding name that intrigued the locals. The story goes that before opening the shop in the late 1920s or thereabouts the family asked the local priest to bless the premises. He could not get his tongue around the Italian surname and mispronounced it Fishers, so they decided to go with that as the shop name. They operated the premises as an ice cream parlour in the daytime while reverting to fish and chips each evening. There is a local tale that the daughter of the family attending a local school was named in Irish, as was the custom, as Marie Ní Iascaire instead of Fusciardi in the roll book, meaning 'daughter of the fisherman'.

Forges and Foundries on Main Street

The quaintly named Dan the Nailor [*sic*] had a forge at 56 South Main Street, reminding us of earlier times when goods were made locally and usually sold within feet of production, even on the principal street.

Wexford Brass and Iron Foundry was situated on South Main Street on the west side at the top of what we call Coffey's Hill. It was run by a man called Henry Hogan and was located behind an arched entrance from Main Street. There was another forge almost directly opposite this, although the entrance was from Henrietta Street. Further south was Osborne's pub and yet another forge operated behind this. To help older readers locate this, Osborne's later became the Goal Bar but this is now also long gone.

Frank O'Connor's Bakery

This firm was established in 1860 and boasted some of the most modern machinery in the world. In 1889 their bread cost five pennies per 4lb loaf. The fine mosaic tile floor is worthy of examination in Boots the Chemist. The upper section of the façade survives with its legend 'Bread is still the Staff of Life'.

Funerals

Until the late 1900s it was usual for both the 'removals' to the church and funerals to the cemetery to proceed along parts of Main Street. These were particularly common in days prior to funeral homes when the removal was from the County Hospital, where it would come down Slaney Street to Selskar and then move along Main Street, turning right at Rowe Street or at 'Coffin Corner' at Bride Street depending on which of the parishes the deceased was from. After the Mass the funeral cortege would leave the church in question and from Bride Street Church would go via Bride Street, South Main Street on to Stonebridge and down King Street to the quay. From Rowe Street Church the funerals processed down Rowe Street, left on to North Main Street and through the Bullring to Common Quay

Street and from there to Common Quay. During funerals it was common for shops along the route to close their doors and if possible pull down blinds as the hearse passed. Similarly, passers-by would stand silently while the cortege passed.

Kearney's at Selskar Street are probably the oldest continuous undertakers in Wexford, having been established in 1925, and they are the only ones still operating from Main Street. Macken's, who used to enthral visitors with their undertaking sign beside that of The Cape pub, have since left that location.

Thinking of the oldest undertakers having been established less than a century ago reminds us that the world of Wexford was very different back then. Looking at some of the businesses listed elsewhere in the book, you will note hardware warehouses and carpenters offering coffins and 'furniture' for sale directly to the public. That was a time when most people died at home with their family. Family members or local women would wash the body and the burial clothes often consisted of a habit (as opposed to a shroud) purchased from a local convent or group (if the person was a member). The wake was organised by the family and graves might even be dug by extended family members if not the official gravedigger. Transportation of the remains to church and on to the cemetery was by cart either with or without draught animals. Therefore the 'complete funeral undertaker' was superfluous.

George Bridges

George Bridges kept Wexford informed of the countdown to Christmas, much as the millennium people did by stealing an idea from Selfridges in London, and from mid-summer his adverts announced the number of weeks left. We all knew that the festive season was really here when George opened his extra showroom down Trimmers Lane and put toys in the shop, usually selling wallpaper and the like further along North Main Street. In the pre-supermarket and toy catalogue days this was the Aladdin's Cave where the wish lists finally took shape.

Godkins

Godkins was a large bakery, grocery and provision merchants with its primary outlet on North Main Street, just south of the Bullring. The premises actually stretched back up to Back Street, where they took regular deliveries of animal feed among others. The bakery provided large amounts of produce that was distributed throughout the south of the county using horse-drawn and later motorised vans. Like so many shops of that era, there were high counters, sawdust floors and clerks wearing white shop coats. As with many businesses, the rear of the premises had started as stabling for horses and later became storage sheds. In the 1960s I recall travelling to the Dublin fish markets on Meyler's lorry and returning with a full load of sacks of meal and the like from Paul & Vincent for delivery to Godkins.

Grocer's Christmas Boxes

This was the subject of a public notice in the *Wexford Independent* in September 1871. It states that at a meeting a proposal made and carried unanimously agreed to discontinue the practice of giving Christmas boxes. As the alternative agreed was to 'enter a subscription for the poor to be handed to their respective clergymen for distribution at Christmas' it appears that an earlier practice was for grocers to give goods to the poor. The notice is of extra interest because it lists the grocers involved in the meeting that year: William Walker & Son; Hayes Brothers; David Faris; Thomas Harpur; John Pettit; Walpole & Co.; Patrick Doyle; Richard O'Connor; William Sinnott; Thomas White; William Wetherald; Gregory Rochford; Jeffares Brothers; Nicholas Colfer; Devereux & Scallan; Stephen Doyle; James Moore; Joseph Lacey; William Armstrong; Teresa Stafford; James Roche and Peter Fardy.

Hadden's

This large store was established in 1848 by George Hadden expanding from a small shop in Cornmarket. It would be the first Wexford store with fixed prices as prior to that goods were seldom priced and as the majority of customers were from the upper class there was generally just some discussion on the price to be paid. With the increase in wage earners fixed prices were required.

In 1858 this was advertised in the *Independent* as the Irish Woollen House (formerly Martha Sparrows) with George Hadden & Co. offering 'good sound articles at small profit asking only one price'. This does not mean a 'pound shop' but rather the introduction of the fixed price.

The first straw hats made in Wexford went on display at Hadden's in 1903. They were known as Tuskar Hats. That April Hadden's announced that all of their six windows would display only Irish goods for Irish Week. Hadden's sold a wide variety of items including waste timber marketed as Tuskar Firelighters in 1937. The advertisement noted that they 'light wet turf' and stated they were 'Eire's First & Best' with 'no need for a draught, plate or bellows'. The firelighters were essential in lighting the often wet turf available during 'the Emergency'. They cost 1/6 per dozen. The waste wood came from the furniture factory they had set up on their property on Belvedere Road, when Addison Hadden decided to increase the employment prospects for Wexford men. Hadden's sold ready-made suits for the men but had a dressmaker on the premises to facilitate the ladies. As was the custom in the mid-twentieth century, staff 'lived in' over the shop and at that time Hadden's had about fifty such staff. The men used one set of stairs from the dining room to the sleeping quarters and the women another. Apprentices paid to be taken on in such high-class establishments and even then they were far from free agents. In Hadden's they were required to sign a book showing they attended church twice each Sunday, where all staff sat together. There was a 10.30 p.m. curfew and their 'social centre' was the nearby Young Men's Christian Association, or YMCA. The shop paid church and YMCA fees but each apprentice had to show work progression by passing an oral and written examination each year. The young female apprentices aspired to be in the mantle department selling French and English fashions.

Hasset's Chemists
This store had the distinction of having a telephone number of Wexford 1 from the 1920s to the 1960s, when the manual exchange was located at Anne Street.

Hat Factory
In an old press cutting – date and source unidentified – we find the following information:

> King Edward has patronised the Wexford Hat Factory and ordered some half-dozen of the light summer headgear which this newest product of the Irish industrial revival in Wexford has put forth. The queen too has given an order for some light garden hats and has expressed herself very pleased with the samples shown to her in Dublin.

The report goes on to relate that the Wexford hats were being purchased in London, Manchester, Liverpool, Glasgow and Edinburgh. It further states 'the war in the east has somewhat interfered with the prosperity of the Wexford factory as many of the fine plats and straw are imported from China and principally Japan and the supply at the present time is practically cut off'. Luckily, the factory had a good supply in stock. Edward VII visited Dublin in May 1904, giving us a rough date for the clipping.

Healy & Collins
This was established in 1914 and was the big shop for Wexford people as it grew in the middle decades of the 1900s. It had a number of departments with some on either side of South Main Street. On the east side was the 'ready-made department', where they sold men's and boys' outerwear. There was also the wonderfully named 'notions department' along with a ladies hairdresser, luggage and jewellery sections. It also had a fabrics department selling dress materials, curtain fabric and 'trimmings'. Upstairs was the 'mantle department' selling dresses, coats and furs. The store closed in 1965 but the memory of the cash system lingers on. It was fascinating to go to this large department store, and buying the goods was incidental to us. When you paid, the assistant did not go to a cash register; she reached up and unscrewed a thing like a wooden jar and placed the money and a docket inside. This was then screwed back into place. A chain – like an old lavatory chain – was pulled and the container whizzed along on overhead wires to the

office. In due time the change arrived back by the same method. Like most big shops of the time, the staff enjoyed an annual reunion close to Christmas and a summer staff outing as well.

Hipps

This was another of the chain stores in Wexford in the early twentieth century. It was at various locations on Main Street over time, including opposite the present Hasset's and further south on the other side. Mr Jackson was manager there in the 1950s. The store was most popular with the 'upwardly mobile' male population in the 1960s and 1970s and was the usual resort for one's first made-to-measure suit. This was a major culture change from the men's father's days when the made-to-measure was usually purchased from one of the many independent tailors dotted around the town. One wonders what that older generation thought of the 'safari-style' jackets and 'bell bottom' trousers of the day.

Home & Colonial Stores (The)

One of the many older multinational shops in Wexford was the Home & Colonial Stores, where a tiled floor was often covered with a sprinkling of sawdust. That was a common practice in shops selling meat at the time as many butchers had a similar practice. It was located opposite the top of Anne Street and was another shop with lots of marble on display, especially where they dispensed the creamery butter. A young man accomplished this with a pair of wooden paddles, with which he shaped the butter from a big mound on the counter. It was weighed in pounds and wrapped in greaseproof paper.

Hore's Stores

The Hore's Stores of today is much bigger than the company started by Johnny Hore back in the 1940s. Johnny had 'served his time' in Coffey's before venturing into his own business. In those days of austerity he started with army surplus, work clothes and some second-hand clothes. In those days before television and local radio most advertising, when not by word of mouth, was in the local newspapers. 'Honest Johnny', as he was known, knew that to get his advertisements noticed he needed a gimmick and he set upon the idea of rhyming advertising. Being too busy to compose the ditties himself, he employed a local bard and sent him regular lists of the items he had coming up on special offer. A small sample of the advertising in poetry went like this:

> Have you ever been in Wexford?
> In that famous labourers' store
> That sells the cream of Yankee goods
> It's run by Johnnie Hore

It's there you get a Yankee mac
From ten to twenty bob
There's hundreds there to choose from
And they're fit for any job
If you've mortar to mix
Buy an English boiler suit
It'll cost you ten and six

This went on for about fifty lines.

Incidentally, about a century before Johnny opened there was a Hoar's Stores (note the different spelling) on the street almost directly opposite but as far as we know it was not related. In January 1956 their advertisement forecast cold weather to last until St Patrick's Day to encourage the purchase of overcoats.

Iberius (St) Church

It is said that the original church on the site was built outside the Norse market gate and there is some confusion as to the exact date of the building of the current St Iberius Church. One source gives a date of 1766, while another reports it being repaired in 1693 and a gallery being added in 1728. It may be that confusion arises due to a number of previous churches of the same name on that site. The first churchwarden is believed to have been Thomas Gilliver and the recording of christenings and marriages in St Iberius were to start from 11 June 1668. There is a record of the congregation purchasing pews for the church in 1716. In 1728 a gallery was constructed to accommodate 'the soldiers of three companies from the nearby garrison and for the poor boys'.

In February 1868 the Corporation paid £5 to St Iberius Church and £5 to Canon Roche for special pews for visiting judges of assizes. The mayor could also use them. In a record of the church vestry from 1831 we get an interesting insight into the organisation and costs. We find that Revd Storey proposed Major Wilson of Roseville as churchwarden, along with Robert Anglin. Messrs Dance and Trigg were proposed as sidemen. The parish clerk was to get £20 per annum for three services each Sunday and four in the week. Mr Mathews was noted as in his fifty-eighth year in the job. Mr Gurley was sesitor, bell ringer, etc,. and was to get £20. The clerk of Selskar was to get £10 and the sexton £5 as there was only one service on Sunday. Wax candles for the reading desk were to be supplied by Revd Storey and tallow (candles) for the congregation cost £3 10s 0d. Painting of railings, doors and windows cost £6 5s 0d, while fourteen panes of glass were purchased for £1 8s 8d. Repairing and winding the clock cost £8 18s 0d, while coffins for the poor cost £5 11s 3d. St Iberius is the Church of Ireland parish church and contains many interesting monuments to Wexfordmen who died in foreign lands. The Major Vallotin memorial is on the wall of this church. Another is to

William Percival, who died aged 21 leading a boarding party off the coast of Istria. The captain and officers of his ship, the frigate *Havanna*, erected the monument. Another monument is erected to Lieutenant Robert Doran, grandson of Robert Hughes of Ely House, who fell at the attack on the fortified Pagoda of Rangoon on 14 April 1852. He had been called to service only five days after his marriage.

St Iberius Church became part of Wexford's ecumenical church history in 1986. When the Franciscans had to close their church to combat dry rot, the Church of Ireland community offered them the use of St Iberius Church to celebrate their Sunday Mass.

Imperial Bar

It was originally the town house of Harveys of Killiane and noted as 38 Selskar Street. After the death of Joseph Harvey the house was rented as a barracks for the mounted police, who escorted the judge to and from the court at the assizes. Mr Lyons took over the house as the Imperial Hotel. In 1881 Parnell was at the Imperial Hotel in Wexford when he responded to Mr Gladstone's speech that dismissed him as an agitator, 'No man in Ireland is good until he's dead. Maybe the time will come when I too will get a good word from an English statesman for being moderate.'

In 1879 the Imperial advertised a hot dinner every Saturday at 2.30 p.m.. Hot joints and vegetables cost 2s but one could also have a sandwich of ham, roast or corn beef with a bottle of ale or stout at the bar. Chops, steaks and soups were also served.

The Imperial Bar was owned by M.J. Kavanagh in 1939, when there were a number of people 'caught on the premises'. One stated that he had been playing cards upstairs with Miss Wickham and Miss Walsh, and just happened to be leaving as the guards arrive. The others were stated to have been guests of a Mr Sullivan, a bus company official, but having a drink constituted an offence. Again, the fines were 2s each.

In its latter years the Imperial was the premier venue for emerging rock bands in Wexford. It was unfortunately burned to the ground in 1983.

Jack Fanes

This was a traditional pub-cum-grocery shop with a little snug inside the door for women before the days of equal pub rights. It also had an interesting lift, which was located just inside the door. This led to the cellar, where, among other things, Guinness was bottled and labelled by the staff, as was the case in most locals of the day with the pub name on the labels. It was a shop that was very popular with country people and those interested in GAA and horses. A regular patron was Jackie Culleton, a very well-known dentist, who had his practice nearby. In 1956 Fane's advertised 'Baby Guinness for the Invalid'.

This picture shows The Book Centre in its original location on North Main Street. The site had been home to Forte's Café, famous for 'orange floats' accompanying sausage and chips meals for clerks from the local shops on a Saturday evening when late closing – 7.30 – saw that extra meal break. (Rossiter Collection)

Jem Roche

Opposite Dun Mhuire was where Jem Roche, a favourite for the title of world heavyweight boxing champion in 1908, operated a public house. This publican/pugilist's advertising motto was 'Only Champion Drinks Served'.

Jenkins

Jenkins operated one of the largest department stores in Wexford in the middle to late twentieth century. This was all the more important as it was a locally owned and operated store that grew organically to eventually take up half a block of prime retail space at North Main Street. The family arrived in Wexford around 1918 when William got a job with Richard Young at 29–31 North Main Street. His first job was selling footwear and he appears to have excelled at this and also seen the potential of his adopted town. When Young retired from the business in 1932 William purchased number 29 North Main and there the 'empire' took root. A few years later he bought number 31 and branched into drapery alongside the footwear business. This was not a great time to be opening a business with 'the economic war' with Britain in progress restricting where goods might be sourced. The emergency then complicated matters further but Jenkins prospered. After William's death in 1946 at the young age of 52 some managers ran the business until his sons were ready to take over. In the 1960s the business grew yet further with four premises being used and with upper floors now converted to retail. They later added an entrance via Mallin Street and would eventually purchase the Methodist Chapel in Rowe Street, adding further retail space. Jenkins was the premier shop in the town at the time, straddling an era of the older international chains that had declined or left the market and the advent of the new chain stores such as Dunne's. For the ordinary 'young fella' growing up in Swinging Sixties Wexford an abiding memory would be going to Jenkins to 'pay on the book', as paying off items bought on credit was called. Little did we know – or probably care – but when doing this we were often meeting Sammy Coe, a man who would do Trojan work in making the history of Wexford known to visitors. Jenkins served Wexford's needs for six decades and it is a tribute to the store that these were probably the worst decades in recent history where poverty was concerned with the reality of large families, unemployment and the actuality of 'barefoot children'.

Joyce's

Joyce's was situated opposite Anne Street. In the late 1960s the front hardware section of the shop employed Pat Sullivan, Joe Fallon and Martin Cleere. We were located just inside the front door selling teapots, crockery, cutlery and the like. Our immediate boss was Pat White, affectionately known as GAA because of his passion for Gaelic games. He had a little office under the stairs that he shared on occasion with the boss, Murt Joyce. The main memory of those early days in Joyce's was of dusting, polishing and rearranging the goods. Then there was stocktaking or replenishing the displays when we had to go to the top floors of the building to the storerooms for kettles, pots, pans, companion sets and a new range of cups and saucers. Joyce's was divided into a number of departments at the time, and up a short set of steps from our section was the paint shop where Padge Reck, and at one time Jimmy Flynn, worked. Upstairs were white goods such as kitchen appliances and also an electrical department selling everything from fuses to stereos. There was also a repair section up there. Among the employees upstairs were Margaret Paige, Des Troy and Tommy Tierney. There was a gas store in Anne Street and another larger one on the quay. Giving an indication of the stock carried, Joyce's also had storage in the old Employment Exchange that once stood on the north side of Anne Street.

Kathleen Doyle presided over another outpost of Joyce's in the China Shop, where we had to thread very carefully among the Waterford Crystal, bone china and other expensive wedding present and presentation wares.

In 1956 their advertised items included: Sprongs for 12s; a Hoover Dustette for 6 guineas; 10-pint aluminium kettles at 12/9 and a Hoover washing machine for only 44 guineas.

Kenny's Hall

It was said to be occupied by Oliver Cromwell in 1649, having been the home of Colonel Sinnott, the military governor of Wexford who surrendered the town to Cromwell. It gained its better-known name when purchased by Colonel Kenny in 1730. He also had a country house at New Fort, 7 miles outside town. Alderman Sinnott took a long lease on the premises in 1848 and operated his business from there. In 1870 Richard Devereux purchased the head rent and bequeathed it to the St Vincent de Paul Society. It was later Woolworths, then Penney's.

Lamb House

This was a shop at the top of Anne Street on the south side and was denoted by a life-size lamb as its shop sign. Con Collins, who had been the Collins of Healy & Collins further south on Main Street, owned it. This would be the first location of a Dunne's Store in Wexford.

Lipton's

We often forget that international chain stores are not the sole preserve of modern main streets. Lipton's was a British chain owned by Sir Thomas Lipton. The Wexford shop was opposite the present AIB Bank on North Main Street. They sold bacon, cheese, sultanas, candy peel and other baking ingredients. It was characterised by its marble-top counter.

London & Newcastle Tea Company

This was another international chain active in Wexford in the twentieth century, better known as the L&N. In fact, for many the name long outlived the business as for years the locals still referred to the Church Lane car park as the L&N car park because the shop had moved there in later years. We can see that it was not always plain sailing for businesses in Wexford from a court case reported in 1944. In it two people (who we will abstain from naming as they may still be alive) were brought to court charged that between 1 March and 18 April they acted 'with a view to compelling John Carton, manager, London & Newcastle Tea Company to abstain from an act he had a legal right to do, namely, to carry on a business of general grocer, using violence to or intimidating John Carton'. The judge ordered 'further detention' but on the request of Superintendent Farrell a sentence of two months in prison was deferred. Unfortunately the report gives no details of the offence other than that stated.

Madam Gaul's

This was the intriguing title of a Wexford shop selling the best in imported ladies' wear. Mrs Healy travelled to London and Paris for stock for her shop. However, the advent of the Second World War caused her to cease such international travel and the shop had to close, with business transferred to Healy & Collins. This was a sad end to what must have been a great enterprise in international couture at 41 North Main Street.

Main Street Surfacing, 1858

The *Wexford Independent* published the proposed improvements to Main Street in November 1858. These included 142½ square yards of flagged footpath from Selskar towards the Bullring on both sides costing no more than £50. The same was to be done 'proceeding towards Harper's Lane' and again 'on the Main Street proceeding towards The Faythe'.

Manchester and Scotch Warehouses

During the research for this book I came across this business in relation to where Corry's later traded. Initially I assumed that this referred to the home city or country of a chain but recent research in a different matter brought a much more interesting explanation. In his fascinating book *Mansions of Misery* about the Marshalsea Debtors Prison, Jerry White explains that Manchester and Scotch Warehouses referred to drapers 'who sold cloaths [*sic*] and other items on credit', and took weekly payments with substantial interest added.

Matt Kehoe's Butchers

This shop was located on North Main Street almost opposite Charlotte Street. In true Wexford fashion the name over the door remained O'Connor. It was a very large establishment with three windows. In the middle of the twentieth century the staff were continually busy weighing out sausages, pigs puddings, chops, beef, pigs heads, pigs trotters and the best of pork. They sold 'Matt's Own' sausages that were famed throughout the county. In those premises young lads could marvel at the deft use of cleavers, razor-sharp knives and saws cutting through bone, as they stood mesmerised on the sawdust-covered shop floor.

Mechanics' Institute

This was founded on 13 July 1849. The rules included 'no papers to be read at fire' and 'no paper to be held more than fifteen minutes'. It offered various classes, a museum and library. The cost per annum for apprentices was 4*s*; operatives 6*s* and others 10*s*. Life membership could be had for £5 or a donation of a book valued over £10. The three-storey house was purchased for £800 while the original meeting to establish the institute was held in the Temperance Hall in June 1849.

Present were James Johnson, first editor of the *People* (he later became a priest); Revd William Moran; Michael Hughes; George Codd; Thomas McGee (who was later a lieutenant colonel of the 69th New York Regiment) and Benjamin Hughes of the *Wexford Independent*. Opinions were sought from Charles A. Walker, Deputy Lieutenant of County, and Sir Francis Le Hunte, Royal Navy, and both were in favour. Le Hunte, who was leaving home at the time, gave £100 and 1,000 volumes. Books were donated by Mrs C.S. Hall (author and traveller) and Mr Boxwell West (native US Consul, Dublin). Thomas Hutchinson (British Consul, Fernando Po in West Africa) gave forty books and some African curiosities, including a bamboo crown used by the King of Bassapo. Ambrose Fortune of Wexford gave a Le Hunte portrait, which cost £50.

In 1852, an interesting competition was held at the Institute. Surgeon Lover gave a series of lectures on electricity that year and the committee decided to hold a quiz in conjunction with the series. Twenty-one people came forward for examination, including three women.

The questions were printed on cards and three cards were given to each contestant. Anyone failing to answer one of the three questions dropped out. This continued until the number was down to five.

These included Margaret Codd, who would later become Reverend Mother of the Convent of Mercy in London and found a House of Refuge there. Patrick Kavanagh, who would become a friar, was also there. William Murphy, who later became master of the Enniscorthy Workhouse, was still in the running as was Nathaniel Vicary, who would join the Royal Navy. The fifth contestant was Master North. Vicary and Murphy received silver medals, while Miss Codd was awarded a set of books, as were Kavanagh and North. It is interesting to note the presence of the women at lectures and quizzes at a time when society was prejudiced against them carrying on educational pursuits.

Members of the Institute were offered half-price admission to lectures at the Temperance Hall in Selskar and in 1858 a popular lecture was entitled 'African Races: their origin, history, characteristics and probable destiny'.

Messenger Boys

Sometimes the title 'boy' was stretching it a bit with these essential cogs in the retail trade as quite often grown men filled the post, and indeed needed to do so. The chariot of the messenger boy was a specially designed and manufactured bicycle that usually had a very large metal frame welded to the handlebars above a small front wheel. Into this fitted a wicker basket measuring about 3ft by 2ft, and 2ft deep. A two-pronged metal stand was fixed under that basket frame that could be lowered to the ground to stabilise the bike when it was stationary. Under the crossbar a metal sign was usually affixed to advertise the retailer. The messenger was the first line of delivery regardless of the merchandise being retailed, from

Paddy Lyons' shoe shop is included here for two reasons. One is the Dutch gable that adorned many of the shops on Main Street over the decades; these may have indicated buildings erected by a particular contractor. The other reason for inclusion is that Paddy Lyons was the first shop in Wexford to provide plastic bags to carry your goods that had the shop name printed on them. (Rossiter Collection)

groceries to clothing. He cycled throughout the town and environs in all sorts of weather and was expected to be on his best behaviour as he was the 'ambassador' for the business.

Naylor's

On 20 August 1845 Naylor's advertised in the *Wexford Independent* the opening of their new establishment 'in The Main Street nearly opposite Allen Street' with the heading 'The Tea Trade – notwithstanding the number of New Establishments of late opened in the above Line and the extraordinary puffing which has been resorted to, to try and force a Trade still the public complain that they CANNOT GET GOOD TEA'. The advert continued, 'he has been induced by numerous friends to resume business here again', reminding the public that he had visited all the English markets to get the best products. His cellars were stocked with the finest wines, which with his stock in Bond in the Queen's Stores he 'respectfully invites a trial of'. His stock included bottled ales, porter and cider and he had 'every article in the Oil and Colour Trade at unusually low prices'.

Newspapers

A number of newspapers were published from various parts of Main Street over the years. In the *Wexford Chronicle* of 18 October 1832 J.J. Emerson advertised as being an agent to collect debts of the late *Wexford Herald*. There is a copy of the *Wexford Chronicle* dated July 1777 in the National Library of Ireland but little else is known about it.

The *Chronicle* reported in 1832, 'A Mad Ass had turned on its owner and bit off two fingers. Some days later it seized a pig and took a piece from it's side. It had to be shot.'

In 1832 the *Wexford Conservative* was printed and published at Main Street 'opposite the church'. It styled itself as 'Protestant and anti O'Connell'.

C. Taylor printed the *Wexford Herald* at Main Street. It contained very little local information, as most news was lifted from London, Dublin and county papers and printed along with local and often international advertisements. It reported some gossip such as, 'A boy went into a field of horses in Drinagh to pick blackberries, he was kicked by one and now has a broken leg.'

The *Wexford Journal* appeared in 1810 published by William Lord, the first issue costing 4*d* and being numbered vol. 5 no. 54, indicating that it might have been published in the past.

John Green established the *Wexford Independent* at 96 North Main Street in 1875, incorporating the *Wexford Journal* that had been established in 1769. In 1858 the twice-weekly publication (Wednesdays and Saturdays) boasted issue number 2825 in vol. XXVIII. The motto of the newspaper was *pro regina et patria*.

The *Wexford Independent* of 9 August 1831 asked that those bathing in the nude near the bridge should swim at an earlier hour or move to the area opposite the King's Barracks. In September it featured a recurring type of advertisement: 'Whereas the conduct of my wife Eliza Anne Green, alias Tims, alias Weld, has for long been outrageous and vexatious, I am compelled to close my doors against her. Not accountable for debts from date 10th September 1831.'

The *People* newspaper was established at 31 South Main Street in 1853 by Edward Walsh and was published each Wednesday and Saturday. It incorporated the *Wexford Guardian* of the previous year and later moved to 1 North Main Street, whose common local name was 'The People Office'. This was the retail office for the newspaper and for the *Ireland's Own*, where advertisements were taken in and wrapped copies of the newspaper could be purchased for posting to friends and relatives aboard. The office led via steps in what was once an open lane called Archer's Lane to the printing works on High Street. The *Wexford Guardian* started at 66 North Main Street in 1856.

Bill Corcoran owned the *Free Press* newspaper, which was printed and published at 59 South Main Street. It was known as 'a farmer's paper' and was often referred to as 'solid as the Ballast Bank'. For about a century it went head to head with People Newspapers for the readership of Wexford. It is mistakenly credited with being the first local newspaper to feature news rather than advertisements on its front page. It did change to front page news in 1969 but earlier newspapers such as the *Independent* a century before had placed news on the front. The *Free Press* closed in 1971.

During the Lockout of 1911 in Wexford the *Wexford People*, in the words of James Larkin, 'gave both sides a fair hearing'. Its editor, Edward Walsh, had a feeling for the underdog and had supported the Land League in times past. The *Wexford Free Press* editor, Francis Cruise O'Brien, changed his position from an initial support for the workers' cause to one of bitter opposition to the ITGWU.
The *Free Press* ceased publication in 1971.

Nolan's

Situated at the corner of South Main Street and Allen Street, Nolan's, with its red-painted façade, was the core of youth culture in Wexford in the 1950s and 1960s. With a jukebox and pool tables it brought a world that had up until then only been seen in the films to the south-east corner of Ireland. It was the place to be seen by your peers, but possibly not your parents. Larry Kirwan captured the spirit in his book *Green Suede Shoes*:

> Many of the misfits who had quit school at fourteen and hung around the town for a couple of years moved to London in search of work. There they would dig tunnels for Mr McAlpine or build cars for Mr Ford until the loneliness got

to them. Then they would take their savings and traipse down to Soho, where they would purchase Technicolor drapes, drainpipe trousers and winkle picker shoes, and return by the boat train lugging suitcases full of new American 45s. They stacked Nolan's jukebox with their choices and lounged around this ice-cream parlour a la Jimmy Dean, while the strains of Eddie, Gene and Buddy ripped through the open door on to Main Street. These echo drenched, bass throbbing, rockabilly anthems were far too angular and aggressive to mix in and be subsumed by the old timey, permissive Wexford musical culture.

Occupations

The majority of those residing on Main Street a century ago were involved in the retail trade or the other businesses carried on in the premises in which they lived. There were also a number of houses with boarders other than the large cohort of live-in staff. These may have been the homes of those having retired from or otherwise lost businesses A quick glance over the census returns for 1911 for Main Street premises also shows a few interesting designations.

Margaret Cullen was a 'private teacher'; George Bishop was a 'sweet manufacturer'; Ellen Furlong was 'of independent means'; Walter Hanrahan was a 'master printer'; Laurence White was a 'farmer'; Katie Murphy was listed as working at a 'graftor knitting factory'; Bridget Bishop was a 'confectioner mistress'; John Lively was listed as a 'bazaar proprietor'; Edward Hickey was an 'RIC pensioner'; Walter Lacey was listed as a 'sailor'; Joseph O'Connor was a 'gas fitter'; John Cullen was a 'telegraph messenger'; Margaret May Kirwan was a 'typist'; Nicholas Malone was a 'pipe maker'; Mary A. Corcoran was listed as a 'newspaper proprietress'; Nicholas Redmond was 'Assistant of Customs & Excise'; George Shudall was a 'van driver'; Thomas Hutchison was a 'mariner'; John Doyle was a 'retired lightship man' and Joanna Browne listed 'income derived from dividends and rents'.

Parades, Processions and Prohibitions

As it came to be the principal street of the town, Main Street would also become the focus of community activities. In Wexford into the late 1900s the principal such activity would be religion related and this was shown most openly in processions on feast days of the church. In fact, religion was a major factor in the principal Wexford parades as well with St Patrick's Day being the parade of the year. This parade has been held continuously since 1917 and prior to that there were intermittent ones. For the resident or visitor to Wexford it may be unthinkable that such parades and processions progressed along the main commercial thoroughfare but in those early days they almost invariably occurred on days when shops were closed and consisted of bands and marching groups rather than with the motorised floats of today. The prevalence of two-way traffic meant that such a procession could proceed either north to south or south to north depending on the church from which it started.

Looking at old photographs, the St Patrick's Day parade seems to have changed its direction from time to time.

In times past, when the town boasted a number of marching bands, it was common to hear the strains of familiar music echo through the narrow street on a Sunday morning. As part of obtaining local authority grants they were required to give public performances and a sunny Sunday morning was ideal for this. It combined the weekly practice with getting new recruits used to playing on the move. The after Mass crowds sauntering to the quays for a stroll after buying the Sunday papers gave them an appreciative audience.

A less musical parade was the 'parade of teenagers' that took place every Saturday afternoon. Having outgrown the Saturday matinee and not yet graduated to the pub, this cohort used the Main Street between about 2 and 5 p.m. something like the gentry used to use Hyde Park or St Stephen's Green. They promenaded, usually in small groups of three or four, up and down the street. The genders were strictly segregated as each eyed up the other, perhaps sometimes getting up the courage for an odd wink or quick 'how are ye?' If money and nerve combined they might repair to White's Coffee Shop, O'Toole's Café or Nolan's, either in their tribes or as fledgling couples, although the latter might be in line from some heckling in such venues.

The parading of small groups was not an invention of the late 1900s. In the early years of that century such groups also sauntered along Main Street but were subject to restrictions and the authorities were known to intervene if a group got too big and split them up, sending each half in different directions. This might have been a throwback to the 1920s when martial law prohibited people from gathering in groups.

Pawnbrokers

In early 1858 Richard Shanahan of 84 South Main Street advertised, 'Highest sums lent on gold, silver plate, watches, feather beds and furniture'. In the same issue of the *Independent* there was an advertisement advising 'the dissolution of the partnership of Shanahan & Quirke, pawnbrokers of 84 South Main Street'.

Post Office

In 1777 there were three post offices in the county: Gorey, Enniscorthy, and Wexford. The Royal Mail from Dublin entered the county only two days in the week, and returned on each succeeding day. The mailbags were never allowed to exceed in weight 'what the Post-Boy's horse could carry in panniers slung across his withers and behind the saddle'. The gentry and men of business distant from the post offices usually had an active footman, who went twice a week to the post offices, conveying all letters entrusted to his care, and was sure to enquire 'was there anything come' for anyone living in a wide circle within the sphere of his activity.

In the late 1800s it was reported, 'We have frequently seen a young woman convey the Royal Mail on foot to and fro between Wexford and Broadway in the one day.' However, letters often lay for weeks before reaching the party whose name they bore. In 1877 there were fifty-six post offices in the county and a mail from Dublin arrived and left twice each weekday and once on Sundays in the principal towns.

The post office was at 59 South Main Street prior to 1894. The opening hours in summer were 7.30 a.m. to 9 p.m. and in winter 7 a.m. to 9 p.m. On Sunday it opened from 7 a.m. to 10 a.m.

The *Wexford Independent* in December 1847 quotes James Rainor of Wexford complaining on behalf of the 'mercantile class' that the English mail for Wexford arrived in Dublin at seven each morning but was held there to be sent on at 'half past eight in the evening'.

Public Houses

The public house, tavern or inn has been the primary meeting place for the people of not just Wexford but of all towns and cities. It is the one place that allows groups to meet regardless of religion, politics or station in life. The number of pubs on Main Street is drastically reduced compared to what it was in the early 1900s. This has come about through changes in drinking habits, the proliferation of 'entertainment' in the pub and the demise of the small family run business. A feature of the public houses of Main Street in times past was that between the Bullring and Cinema (or Harpurs) Lane the pubs were all located on the eastern side of the street. This was because the topography of the town allowed such premises to have cellars where the business of storage and bottling could be carried out at a time when most public houses bottled their own Guinness stout with their individual labels. Many such premises had openings to the cellars in the footpaths outside and in later times toughened glass or metal grilles allowed natural light into the cellars. Interestingly, many people avoided walking on these in case of falling through.

Richards' Jewellers and Watchmakers

They advertised that 'all watch making and repair work was carried out in the shop window in full view of the public'. Their clock still stands, although it has stopped at five past six.

Roche Kevin

Kevin Roche's was another of our South Main Street chippers in times past. As was common at a time when no doubt fish and chips alone would not earn enough to run a business, he had a daytime operation. In this case he ran a shoe repair business in the shop during daytime. This was a takeaway and 'sit down' establishment with the obligatory enamel plates for the latter. One feature of Kevin Roche's was the display of long narrow cinema posters on the wall. These were not as today framed antiques but the current playbills for the three cinemas of the town. Roche's shop was close to both the Capitol and Palace cinemas and many patrons would be in for a feed after being 'at the pictures' and to plan the next week's outings.

Selskar House

This was once number 34 Selskar Street. The Johns family of Carriglawn built it and at the end of the 1700s the grandmother of James Lett, hero of the Battle of Ross, lived there. It was O'Brien's Furniture Store into the late twentieth century before becoming Broader's Furniture Store.

Shops in the Past

In those days, cones and packets were made up for vending loose grains, rice, tapioca, etc. Salt was in slabs and cut into slices for sale, while vinegar was measured into customers' bottles. The working hours were: Monday to Wednesday, 9 a.m. to 7 p.m.; Thursday 9 a.m. to 1 p.m.; Friday 9 a.m. to 8 p.m.; and Saturday 9 a.m. to 9 p.m.

The first time that a shorter working week was sought in Wexford was by shop assistants in 1842. After much agitation they achieved some success but because so many employers refused the demands the gains were lost over the years.

Until 1891 shop assistants worked fifteen hours a day – yes I said fifteen. In that year the Early Closing Association was formed in Wexford. The press, the farmers and some businessmen supported it. An agreement was reached but the shop assistants still worked an average of thirteen hours a day. At this time mechanics and labourers worked an average ten-hour day.

In an address to shop workers in 1892, James Barry reminded them that the shopkeepers of half a century before were slave drivers and were not as enlightened as the owners of the 1890s.

He exhorted the young women of Wexford to look with scorn on any shop assistants who did not support the Early Closing Association. Under the Shop Hours Act children under 18 years of age were not permitted to work more than 74 hours per week.

The following Early Closing Order was adopted by Wexford Corporation in 1906: Monday to Friday, 7 o'clock, Saturday, 10 o'clock.

By 1937 they had achieved an eight-hour day and soon they would get half-day closing on Thursdays. Even in 1956 the Irish Union of Distributive Workers and Clerks put an advertisement in local newspapers stating 'General Public can help by shopping before 1 p.m. on Thursdays'.

John Kehoe, the town sergeant, summoned Mathew Harpur when, on 18 June 1914, his shop was found open at 1.15 p.m. with people inside. Under the act shops had to close at 1 p.m. on half day. He was fined 2s 6d plus costs.

Sinnott's Tea Rooms

This was located at 2 South Main Street and run by Mr and Mrs Sinnott. The final 'S' in their shop sign represented a swan because the bird was in the family coat of arms. The building included a passage to the Theatre Royal in High Street and for a time the theatre sign was on the wall of the Main Street premises. It appears that John Sinnott & Sons were selling tickets for the theatre because in 1885 they owned the Theatre Royal. The passage also led to the studio of Charles Vize, who, as well as being a photographer, was part of the orchestra in the Palace Cinema in the days of silent films. His studio had a display case on Main Street with the legend 'Vize's Dean Art Studios'. At the rear of the premises Bob Doyle ran a small sweet factory, again reminding us of times past when shops sold their own product and long-haul transport and fancy packaging were not even a dream. The passage referred to was probably originally a small lane but there is no record of it. The building had been the property of Hadden's of Wygram.

Sinnott's the Chemist

This was one of many small family chemists in Wexford in times past. People held all chemists in those days in a certain awe and Mr Sinnott was a prime example of this. He was well known for concocting his own remedies for many ailments. One

South Main Street looking south from the top of Anne Street offers us a number of views no longer to be seen. The milk cart selling 'loose milk' from churns is long gone from modern life, while the shop on the left is Con Collins, which later housed Dunne's Stores in their first Wexford location. The bay window above the Wexford Gas Consumers Showroom is now gone. Note the absence of motor vehicles and preponderance of women wearing hats as well as 'young lads' in short trousers and knee socks.

that I recall was a cough medicine that had the magical name of 'hippo wine squills and glycerine'. He was later semi-legendary for a lotion that cured aromatic feet.

Slaney Knitting Factory

William Murphy established this factory with a large number of girls regularly employed at the premises at 81 South Main Street and many outworkers also earning from the business. In 1917 the factory produced hosiery, golf jerseys, knitted coats, underskirts, rinkers (caps), bonnets, undervests, camisoles, corsets, hose, gloves, cardigan jackets, jerseys, football jerseys, cycling, fishing, shooting and sailors' hose, and half hose (socks). They also made silk gloves. Their advertising slogan included 'Goods are made by Wexford girls'.

Stafford's or Stonebridge Castle

The Heraldic Visitation of the County taken in 1618 gives the pedigree of 'Stafford of the Castle in the Town of Wexford' and states that George Stafford, who lived in about 1480, built the castle and hall in Wexford, and his family and posterity resided therein, until the above date. This castle and hall stood on the sea side or east side of the street into the town, between the Stonebridge and Oyster Lane. In the same volume mention is made of Walter Stafford Esq. of the Bridge, and this is the same as the Stone-bridge. After the dismantling of the 'Royal Castle' by Cromwell, where prisoners had always been confined, this castle was converted into a county prison in 1665 and was used to house prisoners during the 1798 rebellion. It continued so until the county jail was built near the West Gate in 1812, when it was converted into a workhouse, lunatic asylum and house of industry. As such it housed the aged and infirm, and also vagrants and prostitutes. Inmates of the house of industry were employed in cleaning streets for a time. It was demolished in 1866 and rebuilt as shops and private dwellings by Richard Derereux.

Stafford's

Stafford is a name that crops up with great regularity in Wexford history. Most young people learning the less than social history taught in the early twentieth century usually associated the name with the attack by Cromwell in 1649 and Colonel Stafford opening the gates to him. They juxtaposed that with the Stafford family residence in the twentieth century known as Cromwell's Fort and put two and two together, making something very different from four.

　　The family has owned vast tranches of Wexford, especially on South Main Street, over the centuries including Stafford's Castle or Stonebridge Castle. In the late 1800s the family was greatly involved in shipping and coal imports as well as malt stores. A map from the middle 1900s shows them owning most buildings between the Talbot Hotel and the north side of The Crescent, as well as land from Paul Quay almost to Joseph Street.

At the corner of King Street and Main Street there was a fine furniture and hardware store belonging to the Stafford dynasty. A portion of this property became the Capitol Cinema, which was the second purpose-built cinema to open in the town. This cinema and adjoining premises, the Granada Arcade (popularly known as Joe Dillon's), which is now an amusement arcade, were venues of popular entertainment. Apart from the showing of films, the Capitol was used as a concert venue. In 1945 the Wexford Theatre Players, whose producer at the time was Kevin Roche, presented Variety Spotlight, starring Martin Crosby and Cecil Sheridan. The queues of people seeking admission to the cinema sometimes stretched around the corner into King Street, and were kept in order by the cries of 'Two Deep Now – Two Deep' coming from a cinema attendant. A notable character of the time was Tommy Swift, a man of low stature who sold newspapers from a little pram-cum-handcart to people who queued at the Capitol Cinema. The Capitol closed in the early 1990s.

Opposite that Stafford's had a grocery and provisions store with cellars. Across Sinnott's Lane they operated a forge, powerhouse, joinery and carpentry workshop with a coal store to the rear and a granulating mill further back towards the quays.

Stafford's also featured in the introduction of electric lighting to Main Street. Before 1921 the company already had its own generating station in South Main Street providing power to its many enterprises. The Corporation wanted to convert from gas to electric lighting and negotiated with Stafford's to supply the power at six pence per unit. The company accepted the contract and the Corporation eventually established its own plant.

In an advertisement in the *Wexford Independent* dated 1848 we find many of the premises that would later form part of the Stafford buildings at Stonebridge were being offered to let by Captain E. Roach of Main Street. They included 'timber yards, sheds and saw pit'.

Sullivan's

Sullivan's was another of the large drapery shops that seemed to be so plentiful in Wexford up to about fifty years ago. In earlier times it had been McHugh & Druhan's Drapery with the traditional shopfront. John Sullivan opened up this area with pillars and a large porch, giving the shop a much bigger window display. It was in these premises – when it was Tyler's Shoe Shop – that the Wexford Corporation set up offices between their time in the Tholsel and moving to the Assembly Rooms in Cornmarket. It was noted in 1903 that they paid £25 per annum for the room and did not use the Assembly Rooms because 'The Gaelic League and Lecture Association used them on the nights the Corporation met'.

Tailors

Although not based exclusively on Main Street the tailors of Wexford town provided great service to the people. Many had 'learned their trade' in larger establishments at home or abroad. They then set up business in upstairs rooms on Main Street or in their own homes. In earlier times it was usually the better off who could afford to buy made to measure suits or coats but as wages improved trade increased. The tailors were masters of their craft and quite often would magically transform an old coat of the mother or father into a brand new smaller garment for a child.

Temperance Hotel

Such hotels were very popular and in almost every town in the early 1900s. Ours was on Coffey's Hill and later became the Delph pottery, second-hand book and comic emporium of Maggie Dempsey, whose brother, Peter, was renowned for the pigs' feet and mushy peas in his establishment at the top of Parnell Street. The shop also sold 'cuts' or, as the more sophisticated later called them, Chester cakes to anyone with a penny. As one person has remarked, 'the flies usually enjoyed them before us'. It was in this shop that many Wexford lads first encountered Batman and Superman as second-hand comics sold on after being 'sent home in a parcel' from emigrant aunts or uncles.

Timpson's

Timpson's Jewellers was located opposite St Iberius Church and it is believed that the business was established in 1792. They supplied the clock for Rowe Street Church in the 1850s. Mr Timpson was also a travel agent and an insurance broker 'for house, land and general insurance'. As travel agents offering 'passage to the colonies and all parts of America' they sold passage to New York, Philadelphia and Baltimore with the Inman Steamers for £3. Passage was also advertised to Canada, Buenos Aires, Australia, China and India. They also offered 'fire proof safes', sewing machines and typewriters. They relocated to South Main Street later and expanded to sales of motorcars and bicycles 'by monthly payments', with a discount for cash.

TVRS

This was not the first record shop in Wexford but it was a very important step into modern times. They were probably the first shop dedicated solely to music and carried a wide range of records. Their main claim to fame was the introduction of the listening station, where you could hear a record in private before purchasing. In the other shops selling records, if you wanted to hear a song you had to ask to have it played over the shop system.

Somers & Porter

WHOLESALE AND RETAIL PROVISION MERCHANTS,

BULLRING, WEXFORD.

We beg to invite special attention to the very exceptional value which we are now offering to our customers and the general public in all our departments wholesale and retail.

Our Flours, Oatmeals, Wheatmeals, Yellowmeals, Brans, Pollards, Palm Nut and Cocoa Nut Meals, Pure Linseed Cake, Oil Cake, Cotton Cakes, Rolled Linseed Meal (pure).

OUR SPECIALLY PREPARED LINSEED MEAL FOR CALF FEEDING CANNOT BE TOO HIGHLY RECOMMENDED.

PROVISIONS.   PROVISIONS,

Long Clear Bacons, light and heavy; Cumberland Cuts, "Fowler's X.L.," and other equally good brands; Rib Middles, Clear Middles, etc. Long Cut and Pic-nic Hams, best Ling and Cod Fish.

KOUGH'S AND BUTTLE'S BREAKFAST (IRISH) BACON. Buttle Bros. and Co.'s Sausages, Puddings and Margarines; fresh supplies every week.

Now that the Bacon Market is dear, our Danish Heads at the price are without doubt the best value in the Provision Trade at the present time.

SPECIAL TERMS FOR QUANTITIES.

Lamb Bros. Jams and Marmalade.

We buy in the best market, in large quantities, and on the best terms; therefore can supply the best goods at the Lowest Price.

CALL AND COMPARE OUR GOODS AND PRICES.

(is)

This newspaper advertisement for the long-gone Somers & Porter will give the reader an indication of the sort of provisions our parents and grandparents bought on Main Street. (Rossiter Collection)

Walkers

The abiding memory of Walkers is of freshly ground coffee long before many of us ever tried that exotic brew. That aroma permeated the store and wafted out from 78 North Main Street. But inside and throughout the large premises there were all the provisions one could find in the most modern supermarket. They blended their own teas, and they had cellars full of wine, whiskey, stout and beer. There was a dispatch department and stabling for their horse and vans, stretching down to the quays. Walkers was the epitome of the glory days of retail with its long dark counter, the drawers of spices and the multicoloured bottles of ingredients, all well out of the 'self-service' hands. The staff into the 1950s were hand-picked, with many in earlier times having paid Walkers for the privilege of serving their time. In that period there were strict protocols, including that in the first year the apprentice never spoke to a customer. Time was spent weighing materials (before pre-pack) and stacking shelves.

Looking back at its history, we note that William Walker opened his premises at 76 North Main Street in 1835. His son followed him in the business but it was later owned by Martins of George's Street with the name retained. Business grew and the premises extended. Over the years Walkers built such a reputation that they had orders for goods from such diverse people as a professor in West Germany to the Ursuline Convent in Waterford, as well as customers in California and New York. These orders could be for a pound of tea or two stone of tea. Another was for cheddar cheese of various flavours, 'to be varied every third month'. They also serviced County Wexford with a list of village locations printed for weekly and fortnightly deliveries, and before online shopping their advertisement read 'To ensure prompt deliveries orders should reach us by EARLY POST on or before the day previous to despatch of the van'.

To give a flavour of the fare on offer at Walkers we look at random items from a newspaper advertisement from early in the twentieth century when they offered 'Genuine' French pate de foie, Danish caviar, jars of Cooper's Oxford marmalade, *l'escargots*, cans of turtle and pheasant soup, as well as vintage champagnes. They provided sheets of instructions titled 'The Care and Treatment of Wine', which included suggestions on what type to serve with different dishes. They also gave out recipes for 'Cups & Cocktails', such as 'Gloom Chaser – one quarter lemon juice, a quarter grenadine, quarter Grand Marnier and the next quarter of Curacao'.

At Walkers Wexford people could buy Stork margarine for eight old pennies per pound or Pheasant margarine for one shilling per pound.

Even into the 1950s Walkers advertised 'Caviar in Glass' and 'Canadian Canned Lobster'. The shop traded for 145 years on North Main Street. When John Henry Martin, the owner, died in the early 1950s his was the last funeral to leave Selskar Abbey before it was de-roofed.

The late John Sinnott recalled his days working in Walkers in the *Bridge Magazine*:

I remember all Walkers staff being engaged in the running of several table bars at a very lavish dance occasion in one of the big houses on the banks of the Slaney. It was either Boromount or Brook Hill. Whites Hotel did the catering. There was no beer served only champagne, wine, spirits and cocktails. Siphons of soda and tonic water were popular. The early festival years were busy years for Walkers as many parties were held in private houses. Ice in those days was always outside the drink never in the glass. The bottles would be cooled by ice that came in big blocks and had to be broken down. As rural electrification was only in its infancy the ice machine as we know it today had not arrived on the scene. Walker's coffee beans were always roasted in a gas machine. Staff was trained to know more about everything they sold other than just handing it out when asked for it. Enquiries would be made from the customer as to its use. If the item was rice and it was to be on table as a dessert then Carolina rice would be supplied. Other varieties of Italian or Chinese would be used for other purposes. The same applied when cheese and wine was being served. If the clerk did not know he consulted a famous book called the 'Grocer's Bible' which had the answer to everything. When table wine was being purchased the customer would be quizzed as to what the main course might consist of. With that information in hand the clerk would be in a position to recommend the wine that would most complement the food.

Wexford Classical, Mercantile and English School
This was at Main Street in 1810 and like so many addresses was stated as 'opposite the church', meaning St Iberius. It prepared students for university, the army and the navy. Under C.P. O'Meara it taught Greek, Latin, bookkeeping, commerce, astronomy, the 'three Rs' and elocution.

Wexford Festival Opera
While the essentials of Wexford Festival Opera are staged 'one street up' from Main Street it does impact on the street in question in a number of ways. Although modern Wexford is multiracial and multicultural, the town of the 1950s and '60s was very different. In those years from September onwards there was a noticeable change in the atmosphere of the town in general and Main Street in particular. Strange accents and languages started to be heard, exotic fashion was to be seen. The opera singers and musicians from around the world had begun to arrive and start rehearsals and the locals welcomed them with open arms.

It was in these dismal months of the year that the public houses began to explode into song as well. The famous 'Singing Pubs' competitions associated with 'the festival' were growing in relation to the number of pubs entering and the quality of the performers. Wexford has always enjoyed a rich musical tradition and the competition gave a great opportunity for the many amateur singers to be heard. Many would not have been regular patrons of the public houses but they were welcomed to boost the musical extravaganzas on offer. In those early days there were no guest artistes or 'big band' backing, nor were there prizes for 'swinging pubs'. The human voice was the primary instrument, often without accompaniment and the repertoire would mix faux opera with piety. Tunes such as 'Saint Theresa of the Roses' would waft from the public houses, sometimes sounding twanged to sound more like 'Sant Teresar of der Roz ez', or one might hear passionate renditions of 'Boolavogue', 'The Old Bog Road' or even 'O Sole Mio'.

Another tradition of Wexford Festival Opera was the Window Competition. This has since succumbed all too often to the importation of professionals to dress windows but back in earlier decades the ideas and the implementation came from the staff of the shops on Main Street. It was magical for young and old to traipse the street on opening night after the speeches and fireworks to admire and judge the offerings. Many shops took inspiration from the operas being performed that year but there was the much more interesting option of using the displays to comment – usually humorously – on happenings of the time, either locally or nationally. It was always obvious which were the most striking or funny windows because as one approached the crowds would be three deep or more at them. Kelly's Bakery was usually one of the more popular, possibly because moulding and shaping bread and pastry to represent figures was easier and gave them better options. Drapery

This picture is beautifully misnamed as South Main Street; in fact it is almost as far up North Main Street as you can get. Of particular note is the sign for the *Wexford Independent* on the left. Further along are the once common 'hanging shop signs' advertising seeds. The streets are unpaved and gas lighting fixtures are to be seen in particular above the YMCA door.

shops used the competition to display their most striking items while the hardware shops also made great efforts.

White's Hotel

This was founded as a coaching inn in 1779 and has provided for visitors to Wexford ever since. The present building is 'back to front' as the original White's Hotel opened on to a very narrow section of North Main Street. That hotel incorporated Mr Wheelock's house where Sir Robert McClure, who discovered the Northwest Passage, was born. A function room within the hotel commemorated him. In 1832 Wheelock's was advertised as a 'gunpowder office'. William Balfe the composer lived for a time in a house opposite the hotel. His opera *The Rose of Castil* was one of the first featured in the Wexford Opera Festival. In an interesting advertisement in the *Wexford Herald* of 3 October 1808, people were invited to 'leave their names at the bar of White's Hotel' if they wished 'to dine to celebrate Mr Ogle's birthday'.

In 1860 we find that White's Hotel is the starting point for coaches to Dublin, among other places north and south. The Dublin journey was by coach to Wicklow before boarding the train. The cost was 'outside (coach) and second class (train) 10 shillings' up to 'inside and first class 17 shillings'.

White's Hotel in the 1960s:

When a night out meant a trip to White's Barn. That was in the days before disco killed the live band and we in Wexford made the weekly or twice weekly pilgrimage to the local equivalent of the Knock Marriage Bureau. Back in those heady days White's was the epitome of cool. It was also a one-stop-entertainment shop. There was the Shelmalier Bar for the cosy drink at an open fire – it later became the library and is now destined for refurbishment. Parallel to it you could go in for dinner, not that most of us could afford it. No, we usually repaired to Main Street door and the fantastic coffee shop. Once more the open fire was a feature with the enigmatic painting above. Did that guy have three legs? How that coffee shop survived is a mystery. It was always packed but how we could make that coffee or coke last. Margaret must have had the patience of Job to put up with us. For the ballad lover there was The Long Room where the Aran sweater brigade could enjoy rousing folk and rebel songs. But the main feature was The Barn. Here we danced, drank – usually coke – and eyed the members of the opposite gender. The entrance was up the corridor under a glass roof. Coats were handed in at the cloakroom where the raffle ticket was pinned on and the other number safely stowed in an arse-pocket. Then on to the ticket office and the seven and six or later ten bob admission price was paid, under the watchful eye of the set of bouncers. Then you entered that other world. Dark timbers, red leatherette seats and the smell of drink. But the more important sense was hearing. The air pounded to music and you could feel it vibrate in the floor as

you passed the stage on your left. You might decide to go up on the balcony above
the band to get a bird's-eye view of the inhabitants. Arriving early you were most
likely to hear The Supreme Seven, The Visitors or occasionally The Travellers.
These were the local support bands that entertained for the first two hours and
we all knew most of the members from the 'day jobs'. I remember Jimmy Flynn
the guitarist extraordinaire – he was from my home turf of Bishopswater and
I also worked with him for a time in Joyce's Hardware. By coincidence I also
worked with vocalist Dermot Kelly in the *Free Press*. Other locals entertaining us
included Michael Holman, Tommy Hore, Dermot Kelly, John Lappin, Michael
Kelly, Don Sadler and Pierce Turner among many others whose names will leap
to the minds of anyone reading this. Then there were the national acts like Tweed
and The Conquerors and, of course, international stars like The Move and The
Tremeloes – we were part of a great circuit back then.

Dancing was always the primary activity followed by matchmaking and then
drinking. Unfortunately, at times The Barn resounded to fisticuffs and sadly there
was seldom a night without a row or fight in the latter years.

Woolhead's

In times past we often wondered at the juxtaposition of Woolhead's and Woolworths
side by side on South Main Street, and thought maybe the former was cashing in
on the name of the latter. In fact, it was pure coincidence. The Woolheads came
to Wexford from Dublin in the 1920s and soon Mrs Woolhead opened a fruit and
confectionary shop paying rent of 15s a week for the shop with extra for the room
with a sink and toilet 'out the back' to Frank Cullimore. Over the years she saw the
profits from such products diminishing and looked around to diversify. She started
to import little ornaments with scenes of Wexford printed on them, as well as small
jewellery pieces. After the war, or Emergency, the shop became what most living
Wexfordians recall, the toyshop. But this was not your chain store toyshop, it was
a family run business with all the ingenuity required to make it profitable coming
from family members. In a newspaper interview some years ago Mrs Woolhead's
daughter, Jean, recalled the task of attaching small Easter eggs to toys for that season
of good sales. She told of her mother's preference for toys such as cowboy outfits,
guns and Airfix models ahead of the increasing prevalence of battery operated
toys that took away the imagination. A sad reflection on the 'good old days' is her
recollection of sitting in the shop until midnight on Christmas Eve to ensure that
no merrymakers heading home broke the window; perhaps they had forgotten to
buy that present for someone special. Her recollection was also of sailors buying
turquoise plasticine; apparently they used it when they were constructing their
ships in bottles.

Woolworths

This international shop came and went in Wexford in less than fifty years. When it was there it was magical; it was a shop with origins in the almost mythical USA. It introduced the idea of limited self-service in many sections – there was always the assistant behind that wide counter. The big thrill was the wide variety of goods on offer under one roof and the amount of gadgets and novelties. Soft-whipped ice cream cornets – we did not say cones back then – were a great attraction just inside the door. It was there that most of us encountered a 99 when a flake was inserted or having a choice of 'hundreds and thousands' or strawberry syrup on the cornet. It was Sinnott's in earlier times, although it was run by a Mr Gaul, whom Jim Jenkins recalled 'looked like a cheerful undertaker', which he was. The coffins were assembled and stored to the rear of the premises, which reached to Crescent Quay. At the front a hanging sign identified the shop with a large key, presumably advertising it as a locksmith among other things. This would have dated back to the days of illiteracy as an aid to identifying a shop and its goods.

Xtra

During research one comes across some items that cannot be traced to addresses or people but rather than discard information that could prove valuable or interesting to others we will include them here:

In 1859 Thomas Prendergast opened his Book, Stationery & Fancy Warehouse 'next to Mesdames Corish and Hughes on Main Street'.

Davies Photographic Rooms on North Main Street advertised for an errand boy and 'only those with character references need apply'. The owner offered photographs 'taken in seconds' and could be 'coloured to life'.

George Carroll offered tickets to Bristol via Tenby with cabins for 31/6 return. The sailings were noted for one day each week of the following month in 1859, with times obviously determined by the tides in the harbour going at 6 a.m. the first week, 1.30 p.m. the next, noon the following week and then 6 a.m. again.

Wexford people considering emigrating to Canada were advised of the following:

Most welcome were 'capitalists of all classes'; farmers with £50 or more; agricultural labourers; boys and girls over 12 years 'brought up to industry' and tradesmen and mechanics but not 'without capital'. They did not want office clerks or shopmen.

An old fanlight used to allow light into the hallway of a Wexford building; it differs from many commonly seen in the 'lantern' style protrusion. This was used to give slight illumination outside the door using a candle inserted there. (Rossiter Collection)

YMCA

We often forget the importance of organisations such as the Young Men's Christian Association in times past, but the fact that their building dominated the North Main Street for more than a century should allow us appreciate it all the more.

An indication of its importance can be gained from a report in the *Wexford Constitution* of 5 December 1862. Under the heading 'Miracles and Prophecy', they reported that for this lecture by Revd John Hall of Dublin 'the hall was filled in every part'. The report goes on to note, 'amongst the audience we noticed nearly all the Protestant Gentry of the town and immediate neighbourhood'.

3

Occurrences

—ᴔᴔ—

While we see Main Street simply as a commercial and retail entity today we must realise that it was not always so. Looking at reports and maps of the town in the later seventeenth century we find no mention of a Main Street simply because there was no such thing. Parishes and wards largely defined the town with a number of lanes noted. To bring alive a street (or streets) we will look at as many instances as we can uncover of events and incidents that occurred on what we now know as Main Street. This will include historical events, parades and murders, but also we will record unusual – at least to a twenty-first century reader – shops and services in the years they opened or were advertised. As often as possible we will retain the wording and spelling as these are best suited to giving the reader a feel for the town at the times in question. Some will be very short notices while others, where we can uncover them, will have longer narratives.

1634
Sir William Brereton gives an interesting view of the town a few years before Cromwell. In Wexford he lodged 'at the sign of the windmill', in the house of Paul Bennett. In the days of great illiteracy, signs and symbols were used instead of shop names. He reported 100 sails in the harbour but the vessels were 'much in decay due to the failure of the herring fishery'. There are also references to quays or interest in quays from every great merchant's house on the shore. This was before the building of the present quay front and therefore long wharfs ran from the current Main Street to the deeper water. At the assizes, Sir John Philpot, judge of common pleas, 'a little black temperate [tempered] man, sat on misdemeanours and trials of life and death'. Devereux and Mainwaring, justices of the peace, accompanied Brereton to the tavern for wine and warned him of 'rebels in the countryside with pieces, pistols, darts and skenes, who would be hanged drawn and quartered on apprehension'. On the street going to the castle one of these was to be executed and he witnessed 'women and others, making lamentations as though distracted and sometimes a kind of tone-singing'. As to the general population, he observed, 'Most of the women are clean skinned and bare necked with a crucifix tied in a black necklace between their breasts.' He recorded that there were many

Papists in the town, unashamed of their religion. He said, 'Mass is tolerated and publicly resorted to in 3 or 4 houses.'

1777

The *Wexford Chronicle* had an advertisement, 'James Cowen, late of Dublin, next door but one to church on Main St, Wexford, cosmetics, accessories and wigs.'

It also listed, 'Alex Stuart, Main St, Printer of this newspaper, list of *c.* 230 books for sale with prices.' And the imprint was, 'Printed by Alex Stuart, Main Street, Wexford'.

1782

We find that Windmills Hill was the execution site for prisoners from the gaol at South Main Street. In August 1782 Mathew Kelly was executed for robbery and was escorted to the execution site by Colonels Jacob and Hatton. There are reports that he confessed at the site.

1792

This is the first reference we find to street lighting in Wexford. It was most likely located on Main Street because the quay front was not yet developed fully. In that year Wexford Corporation made £100 available in its estimates for gas standard lamps. Within a decade the Corporation decided that the cost should be borne directly by residents, although they did spend more than £10 on globes for the lamps. Nathaniel Hughes appears to have had the contract for lighting (and extinguishing) at a cost of £10 14*s* 6*d* 1795.

1800s

The Johns family of Carriglawn built Selskar House at 34 Selskar Street. Sir Jonah Barrington records that the Marquis of Ely, the High Sheriff and other gentlemen of the county were retiring after a meeting of the Grand Jury followed by the customary convivial evening of refreshments when, on passing Selskar House, they heard a maid singing as she cleaned the window. The song sounded traitorous and accordingly his Lordship the High Sheriff and their friends, to preserve the peace and protect the Constitution, forthright attacked her with stones. His Lordship was taken to court and, notwithstanding Sir Jonah's skill for the defence, he was found guilty and fined. It later became O'Brien's Furniture Store.

1807

In March the *Wexford Herald* advertised: 'Linens taken in at H. Boxwell, Hosier, Main Street, for William Atkins Bleach Green, Coolamain. All care to be taken of garments.'

1808

James Boyle, ironmonger, John Street, was selling Swedish deal boards; Cullimores Stores, New Quay, advertised an auction of flour while William Jeffare's, of Main Street, offered brown and white wrapping paper 'at Waterford prices'. James Furlong, Main Street, operated as a brazier, copper and tin smith, and Isaac Wood, Main Street, 'opposite church', ran a copper, pewter and brass warehouse. John Rowley, confectioner and pastry cook, near The Shambles, offered 'all kinds of confectionery and foreign fruits for sale at 20 per cent less than any other house in the town'. Plum, seed and lemon cakes were on offer as well as caraway and coriander comfits, and he added that, 'Ladies and gentlemen may be accommodated with Spiced Beef, Collar and Hams and return what may not be wanted.'

1809

An advertisement in the *Wexford Herald* on 10 May reminds us of the enterprises now long gone that were carried out on Wexford's Main Street. It stated, 'To be let, house and concerns of Richard Sparrow in Main Street. In rere [*sic*] there was a soap house, pans, etc., the materials of a chandler and a soap boiler, and also stabling for four horses and a store with two lofts.'

The *Herald* carried an advertisement: 'Midwife – Frances Stephens, lately of Castle-bridge [*sic*], now residing at Main Street, nearly opposite the church, available for commands.'

1810

Wexford Classical, Mercantile and English School was located on Main Street, opposite the St Iberius church. It prepared students for university, the army and the navy. Under Mr C.P. O'Meara it taught Greek, Latin, bookkeeping, commerce, astronomy, the 'three Rs' and elocution.

1817

The *Wexford Herald* advertised that Francis Atkins (opposite the church) had received a supply of Congo teas; lump and Jamaica sugars, coffee, spices and fresh fruit.

1819

Dr Ryan, the Bishop of Ferns, died at 5 South Main Street while on a visit to the premises.

1824

Pigot's Directory of 1824 is one of the earliest showing the growth of commercial and retail business on Main Street. Unfortunately the street does not appear

Another shop that is long gone is Jim Crowley's. Jim started off in the paint department of Joyce's before opening his own premises. Older readers may get a bit confused with this photograph because Jim had his shop on the opposite side of South Main Street at an earlier time. This picture is interesting in that it shows the brick-built premises, the old windowsill and window. You may also note the separate door to the office or residential accommodation that was once the principal door to a family home. (Rossiter Collection)

to have been divided into North and South and what makes it additionally difficult to locate many of the older businesses is that no house numbers were used. Regardless of this, I feel that the reader will be interested in the trades/ businesses and family names, many of which have long gone from the town. I have retained the original spellings. These are only the ones listed for Main Street and the reader will notice some businesses appear under two or more headings as trades often combined.

Apothecaries: Codd John, McGowran Peter, Ricards [*sic*] James Ricards [*sic*] Loftus, possibly later Richards.
Attorneys: Ball Robt (also 40 French Street, Dublin), Bridson Thomas.
Bakers: Bulger Morgan, Cowen Jeremiah, Crosbie Hugh, Keefe Margaret, Leared Margaret & Son, Scallan Richard.
Bankers: Redmond John, Bullring.

Block makers and turners: Doyle Moses, Walsh John.

Booksellers, printers and stationers: Lord William, Taylor Chris, (*Wexford Herald* office), Wheelock Samuel (binder).

Boot and shoemaker: Colfer Lawrence, Edwards Patrick, Jones John, Kelly Nicholas, Lett Thomas.

Braziers: Byrne John, Cullen Daniel (brass founder).

Brewers: Wickham Michael.

Brush manufacturer: Hughes Anthony, Trigg William.

Confectioners: Robinson David, Rowley John.

Corn merchants: Devereux James, Fitzhenry Robert, Roe Thomas, Stafford Walter.

Curriers and leather sellers: Howlin William.

Earthenware dealers: Backus Jane, Brennan Patrick, Connor Mary.

Grocers: Aikin Francis, Commins Edwards, Connor John, Evans Richard, Frankland Edward, Harper Francis, Hayes Mary, Selskar, Jeffares Shephard, Lambert John, Murphy Lawrence, Murphy John, O'Connor James, Rogers John, Valentine John.

Hardware dealers: O'Brien Julia Ann.

Hat manufacturers: Corish James, Jefferies Thomás.

Hotel: White John.

Ironmongers: Harper Francis, Hughes Wm, Hughes Nathaniel, Sparrow Nathaniel.

Linen drapers: Bennett Hannah, Brown Elinor (and grocer), Butler Mary, Crosbie Mary (and woollen), Davis Samuel, Hore Patrick, Keating William, Lambert Mary, Leared Ann & Co., Meylor Mary, Rea A&M, Sparrow Deborah, Tanner Editha, (and woollen).

Maltsters: O'Connor James, Walsh Philip.

Merchants: Barry Peter (and agent to the underwriters of Liverpool and London), Selskar, Barry James, Brenan Thomas, Cardiff Matthew, Devereux Richard, Doyle Thomas, Gafney Timothy, Herron Thomas, Jones Richard, Roach John, Stone Bridge, Roche Thomas, Jnr, Walsh Phillip, Walsh John, Whitty Nicholas.

Milliners: Devereux, French Catharine, Gifford Eliza, Lett Hannah Maria.

Nursery and seedsmen: Boston Mary and Harpur James,

Physicians: Biggs Benjamin, Selskar, Boxwell Ambrose (member of the English and Irish College of Surgeons, Accouchier★ and surgeon to the County Infirmary), Cardiff Robert, Renwick Robert, Excise Buildings, Thompson William.

★male midwife

Publicans: Gregory Thomas, Mason George, Murphy Patrick, Bull Ring, Pitt Mary, Stafford Anthony.

Saddlers: Gainfort Richard.

Soap boilers and tallow chandlers: Jeffares Rebecca, Jeffares Shepherd, Ryan Patrick, Valentine John, West Enoch.

Spirit merchants: Evans Richard, Bullring, Harper Francis, O'Connor James.

Tailors and drapers: Coghlan William, McIlroy Daniel, Sinnott James, Wickham John.

Tanners: Donnelly Patrick.

Timber merchants: Allen Robert, Eakins Walter (and window glass).

Tobacconists: Harper Francis, Meyler Robert.

Watch and clock makers: Hatchell Nicholas, Higginbotham Joseph.

Wine and spirit merchants: Atkin Francis, Hughes William, Martin and Beatty.

Woollen drapers: Connolly Murray, Crosby Miles, Fortune Moses, Furlong Peter, Lett Thomas, Walsh James.

Miscellaneous: Devereux Nicholas, surgeon, Hogan John, coach proprietor, Selskar Street.

Howard Stott, wire machine maker.

Hughes John, glass dealer.

Keating, Pat, flax and hemp dealer.

McEvoy James, governor of the house of industry and lunatic asylum.

North Main Street approaching the Bullring shows in the centre the gable that was built there when the Tholsel was removed. On the left was John L. Doyle's newspaper shop and Frank O'Connor's bakery. We note that the street is now concreted and cars have made their appearance, while the metal pole carries electric current for street lighting but horse-drawn deliveries are still taking place.

Redmond Phillip, conveyancer, etc., Selskar.

Rudd William, ship and revenue broker, Selskar.

Timpson Timothy, silversmith, Main Street.

Walsh J.W., auctioneer, Main Street.

1830

Peter Furlong advertised in the *Wexford Independent* as being on 'Main Street, next door to Stamp Office, within 1 door of Anne Street'. John Devereux advised customers of his location 'between Church and Bullring' selling teas, snuff and spices.

1831

Stafford's Castle near Stonebridge was a jail until the new jail at Spawell Road was built. By 1831 it had become a house of industry and insane asylum to provide shelter for beggars, prostitutes and the insane. The poor were allowed keep half of any earnings, vagrants none. It was financed by subscriptions from the local gentry with members paying £3 per year. Inmates were also used to raise revenue. Until 1847, the inmates were street cleaners with the house being paid £10 per annum – remember this was the era of animal-drawn transport with street cleaning being quite a messy occupation. The annual subscription from Thomas and Charles Walker (Belmont) was £3 in 1831.

In this year Prices 'old established book and stationery office' was advertised on Main Street 'a few doors from the Bullring'. It was also 'agent for Butler's Medical Hall, Dublin'.

1832

The *Wexford Chronicle* reported: 'A special meeting of the governors of the House of Industry and Insane Asylum decided that due to the increase of cases of Asiatic Cholera in the past few days better treatment of mendicants was needed. In future a good breakfast was to be provided with meat for dinner on 3 days each week and boiled bread and milk for supper.' Among the reported deaths that week were William Westnot aged 87; Israel Daly (84); Catherine Scott (68); Mary Cloak (68); Robert Rowe (80), all from cholera.

William Powell of the Italian Warehouse advertised in the *Wexford Chronicle* that he had a Christmas supply of new fruit, raisins, currants, figs and nuts. He also advertised foreign cigars and Foates snuff.

1834

Henry Inglis, writing in 1836, recalled a visit to Wexford two years earlier:

Wexford consists of one very long and very narrow street, and a quay running parallel to it, and of nearly equal length; together with a few short side streets, somewhat wider than the main street, and not so much the resort of business. There are many good shops in Wexford, and I heard no complaint of want of trade; and the best illustration I can give of the comfortable position of the people of Wexford is that, during the two days which I spent in the town, I was not once asked for charity. Wexford is a cheap place of residence. When I visited it beef was 4d. per lb., mutton 5d., veal 2d., pork 2d., fine chickens 1s. a couple, and butter 9d per lb. A fine turkey may be bought during the season for 3s, and other poultry in proportion; and there is a very plentiful and cheap fish-market.

1836

With a Catholic mayor, Wexford was still a town of the British Empire, and an important person of the empire visited in 1836. The Earl of Mulgrave, Viceroy of Ireland, arrived at the courthouse on the quay accompanied by a company of Hussars. A number of cannon from a private collection of Grogan-Morgan of Johnstown Castle fired a salute on the quay. The Viceroy then paraded along the waterfront, past the gasworks, up New Road (Parnell Street) to the Faythe and back along Main Street. After tea at Bettyville, now Wexford Racecourse, he attended a banquet at the Assembly Rooms, Cornmarket. The Earl left Wexford the next morning.

1837

A document from 1837 regarding residents of Wexford wishing to have the vote gives us a further list of people resident on Main Street.

This is one of many decorative motifs that appeared on the surrounds of Wexford windows in times past. Today very few people look above the current shop signs and they can often miss these relics of a past generation. (Rossiter Collection)

The following residents made a claim (as well as many others) to register as voters for the election to be held on 23 June 1837:

Kehoe, Peter, Main St Wexford, House merchant
Lee William of Selskar, Pawnbroker
Barry James, Main St Shopkeeper & Householder
Doyle Thomas, Bullring, Gentleman & Householder
Maddock James Main St, Shop and Baker & Householder
Murphy George, Main St Shop and Grocer & Householder
Redmond Francis, Main St, Shopkeeper & Householder
Redmond Patrick Main St, Shopkeeper & Householder
Roach Michael, Main St Shopkeeper & Householder
Redmond Francis Main St, Shopkeeper & Householder
Stafford James Main St, Shoemaker & Householder
Walsh John Main St, Coach Agent, Shopkeeper, Freeman
White Francis, Main St, Shopkeeper & Householder

1842

J.G. Kohl, a German traveller, visited Wexford in 1842 but has nothing to say about Main Street, indicating it as being primarily residential:

Wexford, which I viewed the next morning, is an old town, with narrow streets and small houses. The only new, broad and handsome street is the Quay, which runs along the bay, called Wexford Harbour. On the whole, a tolerably clear idea may be formed of an Irish town of the present day, by conceiving it to be composed of the following elements: a number of goodly buildings, a similar number of ruined dwelling houses, a suburb-quarter of miserable huts, some new well-built national and infant schools, some old and some quite modern Catholic churches, a fever hospital, an extensive fortress-looking workhouse, and, lastly, perhaps, some barracks for soldiers.

1843

A report published in the *People* in 1896 regarding trades organising in 1843 reminds us again that Main Street was not yet the major focus of trade in Wexford if we look at the business addresses. 'In 1843 the were Messrs Nicholas Campbell, rope maker, The Faythe; Tom Hynes, hatter, John Street; James Clancy, painter, Old Pound; Nicholas Brien, baker, John Street; George Codd, shoemaker, George Street; Henry Donohoe, shoemaker; and manufacturers who worked with their own family, and employed from two to six men. These included Mr Hynes, John Street; Mr Burke, Laffan's Lane; Messrs. Whitmore and Jones, Church Lane, and Mr Gurley of The Old Pound.'

1846

This year is interesting in that it gives us a very good idea of the commercial activity of the town as it grew from the medieval into the modern.

According to *Slater's Directory* of 1846, Wexford had seven apothecaries (chemists in later years) and all were located on Main Street, including the Bullring. There were seventeen bakers on Main Street and five booksellers. Eight out of twenty boot and shoemakers were located on Main Street, giving us the sense of the town before the 'ready-made shoe or boot' became common, as were the two braziers and tinsmiths of the town. No butchers were listed on Main Street as all were in the old market, Anne Street or New Market off the Bullring. The town is also listed as having such diverse and now lost trades as coach and jaunting car builders, corn merchants, cutlers, glovers, gun makers and livery stable keepers. Most of the twenty-eight grocers were based on Main Street, as were the hatters, ironmongers and leather sellers. Of nineteen linen drapers and haberdashers, sixteen had Main Street addresses. Two of the four nail makers were on Main Street. There were forty-one public houses in Wexford in 1846 but only nine had Main Street addresses – this probably reflects the commercial rather than social aspect of the street. Other interesting entries that year listed for Main Street include Patrick Browne's Temperance Coffee House; Charles Byrne clothes renovator; William Trigg brush maker; Robert Titus Ryke 'miniature painter' and William White 'soda water, lemonade and ginger beer maker'.

1851

On 6 November 1851 Wexford Corporation resolved that the portion of the Tholsel called 'the Black Hole' used by fish women for selling herrings be paved and whitewashed.

1852

Two John Street men, John Brien, a cobbler, and his mate Henry De Roche, were reported to have placed the first picket in Wexford on Taylor's of Main Street in 1852 in protest over the importation of foreign shoes. The shop owner took them to court but no local attorney would take the case for the cobblers against one of the Main Street merchants. Eventually a New Ross lawyer took the case and, after a hearing, the judgement was that there was enough business for both imported and home-produced shoes.

1853

Based on Griffith's Valuation in 1853 we find that the highest valuations of properties are on Main Street and the quays, as well as the principal lanes. The latter was due to a high number of valuable malting premises located on the lanes. Regarding Main Street, we can see one major anomaly in valuation, especially when compared with today. The premises on both sides of Main Street between Henrietta Street and Slegg's Lane are valued at less than half that of the rest of the street. The extremes at Selskar and Stonebridge are similarly valued at less.

1873

In this year we find what may be Wexford's first parking regulations. In November a byelaw was passed that, 'No car, cart, wagon or other vehicle (without a horse or other animal being harnessed thereto) or any truck or barrow so as to become an obstruction to traffic shall be allowed to remain on any part of the public street.' A sort of 'loading bay' byelaw also applied, with the aforementioned being allowed 'to remain only for as long as absolutely necessary for loading or unloading or taking up or letting down passengers'. The fine was set at up to 40s.

This detail from an old photograph shows Hoare's saddlery shop with a shoe and boot shop next door displaying their wares in a way that was very common in times past.

1876

Lyons Brothers of 101 North Main Street were selling furniture, as did Shaw's, 87–88 North Main Street, while Daly's in the Bullring had a bakery and Peter Cassin at 15–16 North Main Street had a printing business. J. Buckley, 58 South Main Street, was a hat and cap warehouse, and Martin Cahill, 72 South Main Street, sold manure.

1877

Great floods were reported in the county of Wexford and the tide was very high in the town, the quays and lower parts of the town being flooded, so that boats passed through a portion of North Main Street.

A young woman named Anne Neill dropped dead in Main Street, and newspapers reported, 'She had not been complaining of any illness previously.'

An advertisement for Thomas Richards, Jeweller, 75 North Main Street, gives us an indication of jewellery prices in that year: silver necklet, 10*s*; gold scarf pin, 20*s*; electro-plated biscuit box, 20*s*; claret jug, 40*s*; ladies gold watch 60*s*.

1880

The sport of bowls, now played almost exclusively on the side roads of County Cork, was popular in Wexford in the 1880s. The game involved bowling a metal ball along the road, the object being to cover the longest distance with the least number of throws. The main venues in Wexford were at Newtown Road and on Main Street after dark. The bowls were even made locally, by 'Dasher' Wafer in Foundry Lane, now called St Patrick's Lane. Charles Stewart Parnell visited Wexford in 1881 and dined at the Imperial Hotel in Selskar Street.

1881

At 38 Selskar Street the Harveys of Killiane Castle had a town house. After the death of Joe Harvey the house was rented as a barracks for the mounted police who escorted the judge at the assizes to and from the courthouse. Mr Lyons then took over the house as the Imperial Hotel.

In 1881 Charles Stewart Parnell visited Wexford and stayed at the Imperial. While in Wexford he replied to Mr Gladstone's speech, which had dismissed him as an agitator, 'No man in Ireland is good until he's dead. Maybe the time will come when I too will get a good word from an English statesman for being moderate.' At the champagne supper that night in the hotel the conversation turned to his impending arrest. 'Who then will take your place?' they asked. Parnell paused in the act of raising his glass and said quietly, 'Captain Moonlight'.

In later years, as the Imperial Bar, this premises was a popular live music venue, especially for bands of the burgeoning rock scene. The Imperial was unfortunately burned to the ground in 1983.

Fortune & Murphy, of the Bullring 'opposite New Market', were selling stereoscope slides, birthday cards and whitewood souvenirs of Wexford with views of remarkable places in the county.

1885

In *Bassett's Directory* published in this year we get a contemporary view of Wexford's Main Street:

> Its main thoroughfare begins on the level and runs along the side of a hill, frequently in such narrow limits as to barely permit vehicles to pass each other. At first sight it suggests hampered energies but closer acquaintance with the people and their quiet and orderly methods of business gives to the narrow street an attractiveness which has to be experienced to be understood.

The author is probably the source of the old tales of the narrow streets where one can shake hands with another on the opposite footpath with his remark of being 'able from a window at one side of the street to distinguish the title of a book which supplies Sunday reading for the head of the family in the house opposite'. Such feats were not actually possible but are handy folklore. He notes that there are broader streets in Wexford but they have not 'succeeded in drawing to them many merchants from the old and highly favoured thoroughfare'.

1889

E&A Rossiter of Main Street were selling 'the newest goods of season' including costumes, mantles, jackets and dolmans. They noted that wedding and mourning clothes orders would be promptly attended to.

Myles Doyle at 9/11 Main Street was selling waterproof car rugs and advertising a 'cheap sale' of room papers. In the same year the Leinster Warehouse on Main Street announced the 'final round of reductions' in an effort to clear stocks before 'it closes its doors for the last time at 6 o'clock on May 4th'.

1898

Wexford was en fête in that month as the foundation stone was laid for the Pikeman monument in the Bullring. There was a huge parade and the whole of the town was decorated. A side note of the report of that celebration is that in describing the parade and preparations we are also give a minor directory of the streets and occupants of the period and who lived where in Wexford more than a century ago.

A fine green flag with a harp flew from the Imperial Hotel. The licensed premises of Charlie Fitzhenry had a display of evergreens and the confectioner Miss Devereux had a white flag with a harp and shamrocks. Miss Lymbery had wreaths of evergreens. There was a green flag with crossed pikes at Mr Breen's and

This is taken from Selskar into North Main Street. Few if any of the shops shown have survived into the twenty-first century. Bicycles, short trousers and knee socks predominate, indicating the date as pre-1960s. (O'Connor Collection)

from Keane's to Bridge's a fine arch spanned the street. Cassin's and Hayes' houses had green flags and from N.J. Cosgrave's to the offices of M.J O'Connor was strung the flags of all nations, except the Union Jack. Other houses mentioned are Ryan's, Hore's and Leary's. There were O'Connor's and Carty's and Richard's, victuallers, as well as the tobacconists, James Murphy. Matthew Doyle had flags and the balcony of M. Nolan's was decorated with evergreens and Chinese lanterns. Mr Stafford's had evergreens and 'from the rooms of the Boro' 98 Branch to Mr Willis' there was an arch. F. O'Connor's sported flags too.

From P. Byrne's house floated a large flag. The Tholsel was decorated with the banner and crest of the Corporation. An arch extended from there to John O'Connor's and Coghlan's house was decorated too.

Buildings mentioned include N. Byrne's, P. O'Connor's, William Scallan's, R. Walsh, M. Harpur and Mr Corish. James Kavanagh displayed flags and Mr Godfrey, Secretary of the Boro' 98 Branch, flew a flag from his rooftop. William Busher had a green flag, as did Rochford's. There was a string of flags from Hanton's to Carroll's and James Stamp had another flag flying. The Mechanics' Institute was decorated and an arch ran across to Lambert's opposite. From Miss Rossiter's top window flew an American flag attached to a pike. From Devereux's opposite ran another arch to the window of the small house. Other houses mentioned are P. Furlong's, Hume's and Mrs McCleane. From M.J. Furlong's to Brien and Keating's a banner waved that included the 'red hand of Ulster' and the words 'orange and green will carry the day'. Mr Larkin displayed a green flag and from Mr Ronan's licensed house to his leather store opposite was a neat string of flags. There were displays by Kirwan's and Keegan's, Miss Roche, Whelan's and Byrne's and from Hore's window. A display arched from John Sinnott & Sons to Mrs Codd's opposite.

P. Heffernan's and Jeremiah Hawkins' houses were festooned and flags flew from the *Free Press* offices. Included in decorations were Alderman J. Sutton's, M. Wickham's, Murphy's, Keane's, Morgan's, Stamp's and Furlongs. The Supply stores were decorated and Miss Quirke's had a motto. An arch spanned from Joseph Kelly's to N. Murphy's with a figure of Father Murphy. More flags adorned Ryan's, Cullimore's, Deacy's, McEvoy's, Stafford's, Pettigrew's, Thomas Hayes, victuallers, Murphy's, Doyle's and L. Donohoe's.

1899

The 'High Class Millinery' business of Henrietta Byrne was at 32 South Main Street, while at 105 South Main Street, John Murphy sold 'room papers, window glass and rosaries'.

1902

In November of this year Gainforts of 73 Main Street celebrated fifty years of existence for hand-sewn boots. They filled boot orders from London, Gibraltar, Capetown and the Transvaal.

1908

Isaac Wood (who like so many others advertised his business as 'opposite the church'), was a hardware, ironmonger, copper, pewter and brass warehouse. James Harpur, Main Street, also 'opposite Church', sold seeds. John Rowley was a confectioner and pastry cook with a shop near The Shambles and advertised 'all kinds of confectionery and foreign fruits for sale at 20 per cent less than any other house in town – lemons 1*s* to 1/6 per dozen; oranges, 1*s* to 2*s* per dozen, plum, seed and lemon cake ¼ per lb'. All kinds of lozenges, caraway and coriander comfits were on offer, as well as best English cheeses. Ladies and gentlemen may be accommodated with spiced beef, collar and hams, and return what may not be wanted. 'Baking each day 7.00 a.m. to 10.00 p.m.'

1910

Murder in the Bullring

On 7 May 1910 Wexford was rocked by a brutal assault that would become a murder case with the death of the victim. At ten o'clock on that Saturday night

Coffey's Hill showing the Wool Shop on the left where the Temperance Hotel had been located. Coffey's is on the right. This photograph recalls when St Patrick's Day parades still traversed Main Street. (Rossiter Collection)

18-year-old Mary Anne Wildes was found with her throat cut in a premises in the Bullring.

Simon Bloom, aged 29 and of Polish origin, rented the studio and apartments above the licensed premises of Philip Keating, known as The Cape. Bloom described himself as an artist and canvassed the town and surrounding area selling picture enlargements and frames. He had been in Wexford for about eight years and his business appeared to be doing very well. Mary Anne Wildes lived with her mother, a widow, at 4 Roche's Terrace. According to early newspaper reports of the time, 'the girl to whom he [Bloom] appeared much attached was of humble position'. It was reported that a business relationship was established between them to the extent that when he went to Dublin, 'where he sojourned during the Jewish feast of Passover', she had the keys and care of his studio.

On 7 May John Doyle and a companion named Thomas Lewis of Mary Street believed that they heard moaning coming from the hall leading to Bloom's part of the premises. They opened the lid of the letterbox and asked who was there. The voice replied, 'Mary Anne'. The door was locked and the two men tried to decide what to do next when they observed Mr Bloom coming from Common Quay Street and heading up Main Street. They called to him saying there was a child or someone on the stairs. Bloom told them he had left a man and woman inside. He took two keys from his pocket and opened the latch and 'large lock'. On entering the men found a girl leaning against the balusters [*sic*] of the stairs. Bloom shoved her aside to reach the stairs. Aroused, she moved towards the door. Blood gushed from a neck wound and 'covered her dress and stained a white rose that she was wearing a dark crimson'. She collapsed in Lewis' arms. Lewis carried the girl out and shouted for someone to fetch a doctor. Some men procured a handcart from a neighbouring public house and the girl was placed on it. Carefully and as quickly as possible they carried her on this cart to the County Infirmary in Hill Street.

On Sunday at 2.30 p.m. a deposition was taken from the girl. At the later inquest Dr Hadden would admit that he 'had no hope for her but I had to tell white lies to try and buck her up'. The deposition was taken in the surgery of the Infirmary in front of Sir William Paul, resident magistrate. Her deposition was:

> I know Simon Bloom who is now present. I am and was acquainted with him. I saw him yesterday at the 6.30 train for Killinick. It was then arranged that I was to visit him at his house in North Main Street. I was in his house last night as arranged. Simon Bloom attempted to choke me.

Mary Anne died at 10 o'clock that Sunday night. On Tuesday at 11 o'clock Peter Ffrench, the coroner, opened the inquest in the boardroom of the Infirmary. After some deliberation the jury returned a verdict that Mary Anne Wildes died as a result of heart failure through loss of blood through a throat wound that in their opinion was inflicted by Bloom.

At the subsequent trial Bloom was found guilty and served a number of years in prison for his crime. It is believed that he emigrated to America upon his release.

The grave of Mary Anne Wildes is in Crosstown cemetery and into the present century flowers were regularly placed there.

1911–12

The urban population of Wexford in 1911 was 11,531, of whom almost 5,000 were aged less than 20 years.

Among the occupations recorded were eight doctors, nine writers, two painters and three sculptors. There were eighty-one railway employees, forty-nine printers and eight watchmakers. Twenty-one men were involved in coach building and fifteen shore-based ship's carpenters were recorded. The town had twelve maltsters or distillers and fifty-five bakers. Sweeps and soot merchants numbered four. There were two female brokers and one woman accountant. Two women were engaged in upholstery or cabinet making and one was a brewer, while there was also a female forge-keeper or blacksmith. Another three women were employed as quill or feather dressers.

On 9 December 1911 the *Wexford People* reported that a group of blacklegs, two of them local, were attacked by a crowd on Main Street and had to take refuge in a shop until the Royal Ulster Constabulary (RIC) arrived. In mid-December a further seven 'imported workers' had arrived (from Belfast) to work in the Selskar Ironworks.

On Thursday, 10 January 1912, two wagonloads of beds were moved from the South Station to Brien & Keatings on Main Street that had been acquired by Pierces for conversion into a hostel for sixty blacklegs who were expected to arrive in Wexford. That night the blacklegs, who had been billeted in Pierces factory, were transferred to Brien & Keatings without any reported incident, possibly due to the fact that a major fundraising concert was taking place in the Theatre Royal on the same night. On the same day in mid-January that P.T. Daly arrived back in Wexford and was escorted to his lodgings by an enthusiastic crowd, a majority of that same crowd then proceeded on to Brien & Keatings, where there were stone-throwing incidents that resulted in the RIC pushing the crowd down Anne Street. These incidents were the result of the enthusiasm generated by Daly's return and the arrival of thirteen blacklegs from Carlow earlier that afternoon.

Serious rioting occurred immediately after Daly's arrest on 27 January. The *People* reported that Main Street, especially near Brien & Keatings, was thronged on that Saturday night with 'feelings running very high'. It was considered fortunate that there was no baton charge by the RIC as there were many women and young children among the crowd. Although the crowds were dispersed there were a number of incidents that resulted in arrests for disorderly conduct. A baton charge at Bride Street resulted in John Carroll, a resident of the street, receiving 'nasty scalp wounds'. In early February three blacklegs working at the Selskar Ironworks were arrested for being drunk and disorderly on the quays. They were released on payment of a nominal fine and on condition that they would leave the town. On Sunday, 4 February three blacklegs who had worked the previous week in Pierces, and were from Cork, arrived in Enniscorthy on the 12 o'clock train from Wexford. The blacklegs, three brothers named Carroll, were jeered and threatened by a large crowd at the station.

The date was 7 September 1911, a Thursday. At the behest of the employers, extra police, RIC, were drafted into town to subdue the locked out workers who had been regularly gathering with women and children to boo and jeer at workers imported from as far away as Leeds to carry on the work they were prevented from doing. These 'scabs' or 'blacklegs' were shipped in and housed in dormitories in the town.

On that Thursday the police reinforcements arriving at the North Station marched along the quay towards Barrack Street, where they were to be billeted. This in itself appears provocative as the South Station was nearer the military barracks. During the march they were the subject of jeers and verbal abuse from the

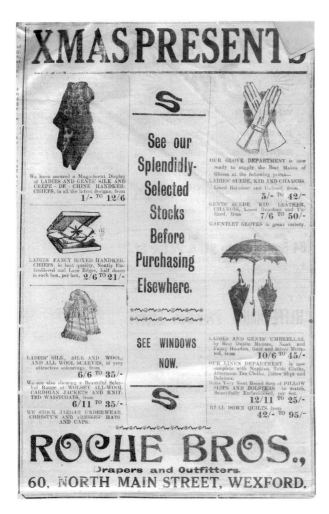

Christmas 1922. When Roche Brothers had their shop at 60 North Main Street they offered these items for the delectation of customers. (Rossiter Collection)

townspeople; there were allegations of some stone throwing. The police responded with a baton charge on the busy streets of the market town. They targeted anyone they thought might appear to be a 'union sympathiser'.

People fled in panic down South Main Street into Bride Street and Keyser's Lane. At times the foundry workers in the crowd stood their ground and engaged in fisticuffs with the police, but fists were no match for the concerted baton attacks. Terror reigned in the narrow streets and one must imagine the scatter of women and children.

Injuries were inflicted throughout the town but the worst of the fighting occurred in the South Main Street area.

An 8-year-old boy, Thomas Whitney, reported to the inquest that on the Thursday night he 'got a lick of a baton on the head'. He said he got it from a 'stout policeman with a black moustache'. He said it happened 'around at the end of Gibson's Lane' and that he saw a man on the ground all covered in blood.

A Mr O'Dempsey [*sic*] reported to the inquest that he had been struck on the arm while holding his 8-year-old daughter in his arms outside Coffey's. He said that the policeman 'ran from the middle of the road on to the path, struck me on the arm'. The policeman is then said to have continued on and struck his wife. On going to some policemen at the *Free Press* to report his wife being hit they were told 'they had no right being on the street at that time'. This was close to midnight after much of the trouble was over. The witness said that there were a few young people still on the street and the policemen 'went up the hill'.

More than twenty people received 'serious head wounds' requiring overnight hospitalisation at the County Infirmary. These included Stephen Sinnott, John Harpur and Stephen Colfer from King Street, Thomas Callaghan, Laurence Walsh and John Boyt (Boyd?) of Bride Street, as well as James Lacey from High Street, and Nicholas Redmond, Mary Street, William Birney of Distillery Road.

Michael O'Leary was not admitted on the night of the trouble and his story only became common knowledge over the following days.

Doctor Pierse would tell a later inquest that he was called to see O'Leary at about three o'clock on the Friday afternoon. He had dressed the injury but did not think it serious enough to warrant sending him to the Infirmary. This would prove crucial in later days as there was a dispute as to how much the delay in seeking medical treatment would contribute to his death from septic meningitis. On seeing the patient on the Saturday night the doctor had him removed to the Infirmary. At the inquest Dr Pierse, who also performed the post-mortem examination, and Dr Stanislaus Furlong attested that although septic meningitis killed Michael O'Leary it could not have occurred in such a generally healthy man without him having received the head injury.

O'Leary, described as 'a respectable working man of quiet and unobtrusive habit', was neither a foundry worker nor indeed did he work in the town. He was aged 56 and lived at 9 Michael Street with his wife Mary, aged 49. With them lived their sons William (26), a messenger; Philip (23), a general labourer; James (19), a fitter (possibly a foundry worker); Edward (19), a printer; Moses (15), a messenger; and Patrick (8) plus daughter Mary (10), the latter two at school. The *c.* 1911 census records the house as having five rooms and two front windows.

On the fateful night he was set upon when he went to buy tobacco after coming home from work in Castlebridge, a nearby village.

Margaret Neill told the inquest that she saw Michael O'Leary 'going down by Bride Street' on the night in question. She stated that five policemen attacked him from behind at 'Joe Kelly's door'. She saw no stones being thrown and said, 'They hit him as hard as they could, harder than you would a lump of coal to break it.' She said they, 'struck him one after another when he was on the ground'.

His son, who worked for M.J. Furlong on South Main Street, told the inquest that he had met his father on the fateful night at about eight o'clock 'opposite Deasey's public house'. He was walking home alone. He informed his son 'he was after getting a beating by the police'. He took his cap off and found his head covered in blood. When he got home, 'Kate Kehoe stuped [this was a common expression in Wexford meaning variously steeped or cleaned usually with a disinfectant] his head and put a plaster on it'. He said that the next day his father 'did not appear to be very bad'. Catherine Kehoe lived at 13 Michael Street.

This innocent man's death caused a groundswell of bitterness against the police. And the people now had a greater focus and a greater alienation from the establishment of police and employers.

Newspaper reports of 'the funeral of poor Michael O'Leary, who received his death blow on the occasion of a baton charge in Wexford', said that the cortège was undoubtedly the largest ever seen in the town. Most houses on the route closed and drew their blinds. St Brigid's Fife and Drum Band preceded the funeral and 'locked out workers' from the three factories marched four deep before the hearse. Union men carried the coffin. The interment in Crosstown had rites performed by Father Owen Kavanagh, assisted by Father John Codd.

Wexford Corporation Finance and Works Committee tendered 'sympathy to Mrs O'Leary on the murder of her husband'.

Ironically the only charges resulting from this 'riot' were laid at Wexford Petty Sessions on 11 October when one man was sentenced to imprisonment and ten were ordered 'to find sureties to keep the peace for having committed assaults or taken part in rioting of 7th of September'.

1914

The headline in the *Free Press* in January read 'The Flying Gasman' over a story about a lady being knocked down on Main Street by an employee of Wexford Gas Company who was speeding on his bicycle.

The renowned Irish songwriter Percy Ffrench was in the Town Hall in April to give a 'humorous song and art recital'. Tickets and a plan of the hall were available at Miss Malone's, North Main Street.

At the petty sessions Peter Cleary of Roche's Terrace was fined 1s for allowing his goat to wander in Bride Street. A labourer from Byrne's Lane was charged at a special court in South Main Street Barracks with desertion and failing to support his wife and children. He had been arrested in Liverpool and Constable Sloan had gone there to bring him back. After the hearing he was removed to Waterford Jail.

Petro Lenzi, an Italian and proprietor of The Very Place, South Main Street, charged Michael Neville, Trimmers Lane, with breaking a window in his premises where he sold 'chipped potatoes'. It was stated that the defendant had asked for 'halfpenny worth on Christmas Day'. Such small amounts were not for sale and when he was put out, he smashed the window. The magistrate said that the plaintiff was entitled to fair play, while a police sergeant stated that the chipper was a rowdy place. Due to problems over dates the case was dismissed. (This may have been a reference to Christmas Day rather than Christmas Eve.)

Local politics continued in this heady atmosphere and the results of local elections were announced in early June. On that occasion a large crowd gathered on Main Street opposite the town clerk's office at 11 o'clock at night to hear the result. There were three candidates for two seats on the county council for the Wexford Town District. Philip Keating got 665 votes, John J. Kehoe 633 and Thomas O'Brien 569. The first two were elected. Mr O'Brien was a Labour Party candidate and when addressing the crowd Richard Corish faced a mixture of cheers and hisses as he extolled the achievement of almost 600 votes. He blamed lack of funds, lack of vehicles and 'open public houses' for the defeat.

Some other interesting advertisements involved money lending. Various companies, mainly based in Dublin, offered loans that ranged from £15 to £5,000 without security. These were aimed at various specific groups. Some were for 'farmers, shopkeepers and other responsible persons on their own signature'. Another targeted clergy and traders with the offer of a loan in secrecy and advising them not to 'borrow in your own town where you and the lender are known'.

This did not discourage Robert Coffey of South Main Street, who offered to advance money on a range of jewellery, guns, furniture, wearing apparel and other valuables. The advertisement noted that valuables sent by registered or parcel post would get prompt personal attention.

This is a glimpse of something very few realised existed for the residences on Main Street. As well as having yards and stables they often also had gardens. This instance was behind 39 North Main Street and stretched up to Back Street, where there was a separate entrance. (Rossiter Collection)

1917

At this time, the quay was not a public road. Street lighting was by gas and a man went about in the evenings and mornings lighting and extinguishing the lights.

Walter Carter of Charlotte Street was fined 6*d* for playing football on the street. He said that on returning from the chapel some children had kicked the ball to him and he kicked it back. The constable stated that Carter had picked up the ball, a football case filled with hay, and kicked it from Charlotte Street into Main Street. This caused inconvenience to people using the street for business or pleasure. Handball playing on the streets was another hazard. Plain-clothed constables were used to apprehend the culprits, among them Michael Grace and Laurence Kehoe at Johns Gate Street, who were playing against the churchyard wall. Despite complaints that there was nowhere else to play, they were fined 6*d*.

In 1917 there were at least seventy publicans operating in Wexford and many of these were located on Main Street. This is an interesting fact in light of revelations in a recent book, *Wonderland* by Steven Jones, which reminds us of the importance of the inn, tavern and public house in human development. This was the first space away from home, church or work where people could gather. This interaction would lead to many revolutionary ideas in politics and business.

1920

In September 1920, forty members of the Devonshire Regiment, stationed at the barracks, ran amok on Wexford's streets. They accosted civilians with demands to know the location of the Sinn Féin Club and, not satisfied with the replies, they assaulted the people questioned. The RIC tried to intervene but their requests for assistance to troops at the barracks went unheeded. Finally the local people could take no more and hit back. Fights broke out on Main Street and at the Bullring, with stones and bottles thrown. Eventually the soldiers were driven back to the headquarters.

1922

The bridge at the Boat Club, then the nearest bridge to town, was blown up and it burned for days. The Mechanics' Institute at Main Street was commandeered as a first-aid station. The military barracks was fired on from a field near Distillery Road, probably behind the C.B.S. More than twenty rounds were fired but there was no return fire. Some of the bullets were found lodged in the walls of Mr W. Murphy's bedroom in Barrack Street.

Sniping on the barracks continued intermittently, and the police barracks at South Main Street (now Dun Mhuire) was also attacked.

A curfew of 11 p.m. was imposed, but was largely ignored by the townspeople who strolled the streets discussing the situation.

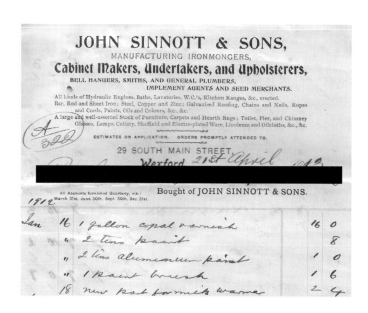

This invoice from John Sinnott & Sons dating from 1912 reveals the varied stock carried and the number of businesses being carried out in a single premises. (Rossiter Collection)

1923

Main Street was asphalted in 1923.

1935

In *Thom's Directory* there are twenty-two drapers and outfitters listed on Main Street, along with ten of the town's dozen fruiterers. Twenty-one out of the forty-eight grocers and wine and spirit dealers were also on Main Street. It is interesting to note the number of female proprietors listed in 1935 such as Miss Codd of Cinema Bar, Miss Dillon, Mrs Fox and Mrs Hore.

1939

In January a number of pubs were prosecuted for having people on the premises after closing time. These were The Selskar Bar, The Cape and the Imperial Hotel. Closing time on Saturdays was 9.30 p.m.

Men employed on resurfacing North Main Street went on strike claiming that heavy work such as breaking concrete should be on a five-day week, not three days as it was under 'the Relief Scheme'.

1946

In October of this year we are reminded of how the Second World War, or the Emergency, had affected people in Wexford by this report in the local newspaper:

Shopping News

While customers no doubt still experience disappointment in their quest for drapery and household goods we are indeed very glad to announce somewhat brighter news for the days ahead. Mr J. Healy, Managing Director of Healy & Collins, has paid a second visit this season to the English markets of London & Manchester where he purchased large quantities of goods, most of which are making a welcome re-appearance after years of scarcity. These include interlock underwear for ladies, quantities of silk and plated stockings, pure wool cardigans and jumpers, curtain nets (fancy and plain meshes) and linoleum floor covering.

1949

Tuesday, 11 October 1949, marked the tricentenary of Oliver Cromwell's fateful entry into Wexford. To commemorate the occasion a procession went from Cornmarket to South Main Street and paused outside Sinnott's, now Penney's, where Cromwell is reputed to have lodged. It then went to the military barracks, where the band played 'Memory of the Dead'. They also visited the Friary and Cornmarket.

1952

Another art form reached Wexford in 1952 as the first ever television pictures in town were received via the BBC in England in that year. The men responsible were John Scanlon and J. Kehoe of the Radio Depot, 77 North Main Street. The pictures must have been promising as Wexford's first television store, Radio-Vision, opened at the Bullring in July of the same year.

1956

In his book *Green Suede Shoes*, Larry Kirwan recalls:

Rock & Roll hit Wexford like a ton of bricks, and little has been the same since. Wexford might have been a backwater in many ways, but it was ever vigilant and super-hip to the changing styles of popular entertainment. Eddie Cochran, Gene Vincent, Buddy Holly and many others now lost in the mists of rockabilly legend were already household names in Maudlintown, White Rock and Selskar before the ink had dried on their record contracts. A riot broke out in the Capitol Cinema when *Rock Around The Clock* played there in 1956. The action spilled out on to the Main Street where Teddy boys and girls continued to jive and gyrate to the strains of Bill Haley and his Rockets. Flick knives and broken bottles were waved in the faces of the *Garda Siochana* who tried to restore order. The town's elders wrung their hands in despair, while questions were asked in the local papers about this new generation and the music that was driving them mad.

1960s

At the corner of Stonebridge Lane where the motor factory shop now stands there was once a smaller shop. Initially it had been Cullimore's but many who had their school days in the 1960s will remember it as Morgan's. Mister Morgan had been in management in Pierce's before branching into the retail book and stationery trade. The shop always seemed cluttered with no law or order on the contents. He did not carry much in the book line, but then very few did in those days before the really cheap paperback and the specialist bookshop. Andy Nolan had a vegetable shop almost opposite at one time and there was another such shop on the western side. I think it was called the General Stores but for some reason the locals had their own name for it from a popular television cartoon series. An indication of the popularity of music-making and being in a pop group is attested by the fact that Noel Randall could open a retail music shop here.

Hayes (we pronounced it Hayeses) and Kavanagh had a popular bicycle shop along here at a time when for most of us two-wheeled transport was as advanced as we might aspire. They also sold fishing bait. Further along was Kelly's Dairy and then McGrail's drapery shop. On the other side we had Eddie Slevin's electrical contractor and retail lighting shop. Paddy Carey's pub was opposite Bride Street and Barry's fish shop was beside it selling the best of Rosslare herrings. Broaders, Travers, Bugler Doyle's and the like were pub names opposite that corner. I recall

This shot captured at the rear of a seaward side premises on North Main Street in about 2003 is another reminder of the enclosed gardens associated with houses on this street. This gate may once have opened on to a strand or jetty prior to the building up of the quay front in the early 1800s. (Rossiter Collection)

going into one of them – no naming which – at lunchtime for a sandwich and the barman popping out to buy a sliced pan to facilitate the transaction.

Malone's Fish Shop was at the corner of Oyster Lane. He usually had a big Delph plate in the window – blue willow pattern I think – and more often than not the family cat was perched on it sunning herself.

On the Bride Street side was Coffin Corner with a three-storey redbrick town house. I cannot recall it as a residence but do remember one of the many Tontine societies using the lower front rooms every Saturday to collect the money. Next door used to be Denis O'Connor's studio, where many a scabby knee was photographed in a short-trousered First Holy Communion suit. Above the studio lived Marty Murphy, the brain that propelled many a young Wexford man into business or accountancy. He was the teacher of bookkeeping and business methods in the CBS Secondary School in Green Street. He always wore a three-piece suit and a hat outside class and was forever enquiring after Canon Murphy out in Glynn from any pupils from that area.

Aidan Kelly had a butcher shop next door and I seem to recall Tom Furlong – later of the Bullring – working for him. Beside this was the public convenience at the corner of the appropriately named Mann's Lane. A man nicknamed Sugar Al worked there in the days of fully attended toilet facilities.

The Pettit's retail empire started in a shop across the road from here at Oyster Lane. It grew from a small retail unit in 1947 to a mini supermarket before expanding to pastures new and eventually closing the South Main Street branch.

Then came the parish hall – official name Dun Mhuire. This was our Mecca for pantomime, dancing, record hops, bingo (for the Ma), jumble sales, Tops of the Town, concerts by international stars, drama festival in Lent when dancing was prohibited and a hundred other entertainments including roller disco. Upstairs there were meetings of the Catholic Girls' Club, the Legion of Mary, Alcoholics Anonymous, the Holy Family Confraternity Band and others.

Next door was Alf Cadogan's, where you could get electrical goods, bicycles, tricycles and a multitude of other items. It later became Jim Crowley's Paint Shop. Opposite there were shops such as Kirby's chemists and Kelly's hair salon – there was a shop out front that you passed through to get the 'short back and sides' that was obligatory before the Beatles and other mop cuts became popular.

Johnny Murphy's Goal Bar was also on this stretch of street and was a very popular location for GAA aficionados. One older institution here was Kevin Roche's, the old-style chip shop for take away or sit-in after a night at the pictures. It was chips, fish, mushy peas, pig's feet, minerals and little else, served in newsprint or on enamel plates. The long playbills for the three cinemas provided the reading material.

Coleman Doyle began his expansion along here with a catchphrase for those seeking anything from a needle to an anchor of, 'If I haven't got it I will get it for you.'

Across the road, the Lowney juggernaut shifted into gear from small beginnings to occupy a huge store that stretched from Main Street almost to the quay at a time when most shops were about a 'house deep'. Their furniture provided the necessities and home comforts to thousands of Wexford couples starting out on married life, often 'bought on the book'.

Other pubs in this corner included Heffernan's and Nick Murphy's, the preferred haunt of the *Free Press* staff after work or 'the going away or getting married do' when the 'wallop a notes' was handed over amid the flowing drinks. Across Cinema Lane was Eddie Hall's pub and directly opposite Hall's was Shudall's sweet shop. I recall this little shop of about 8ft by 20ft with a counter down the right as you entered and a bench or form on the left wall under a mirror. An elderly lady owned the shop but most of the service was by Angie Molloy. It was the place to stock up on sweets when heading for the Cinema Palace.

Coffey's was a Wexford institution in the 1960s as it had been for decades. In 1939 Coffey's offered 'the greatest bargains ever experienced', including pianos, cycles, prams, clothing and diamond rings. It was the place for shoes, boots, clothes, bedding and nursery requisites. Initially presided over by Herbie and later his son Ray, it was one of the friendliest stores you might enter.

Up Coffey's Hill – which had its own tune composed for the Boys Band – was Wallace's. This was higher class tailoring with measuring, fitting, etc., and was the place for that special suit. Bucklands was on the same side in my day, although I understand it had started life on the other side of South Main Street. May and Ita were the occupiers in the 1960s and, again, it was a very small shop. As you entered there were newspapers to your right, then weekly comics and magazines on the wide counter with sweets underneath. The books were shelved to your left. To the rear were the 'classy comics', the Classic Illustrated, Dell, DC Comics and the sixty-four-page War Library range. Here we delved into the adventures of Batman, Superman and the other superheroes of the magical USA. Such comics were for special occasions or when we had that extra few bob after doing a few 'messages'. The bread and butter comics were *The Topper, Beezer, Dandy, Beano* and the like that the parents usually bought on a weekly basis as a regular treat. There was a science to this purchasing; it had to be controlled so that there was a swap market potential so parents were usually instructed what to buy and what to avoid because one of our friends had it on order. Commodity trading had nothing on us in those days.

Beside Bucklands was the Singer sewing machine shop and opposite was a greengrocer on the corner of Henrietta Street. Yet another homegrown retail giant started out on this bit of South Main Street in the 1940s, Johnny Hore's. Nolan's, on the corner of Allen Street, was a hub of teenage activity in the early days of teenagers. It had a jukebox and a pool table and was a sort of unofficial youth club on most days and nights of the week behind its red façade.

Paddy Lyons was a shoe shop that is said to have introduced the printed plastic carrier bag to Wexford. Woolworths has been recorded before but what about the shop next door – similar name but no relation. That was Woolhead's, one of the major attractions for young and old throughout the year but especially at Christmas. Its Aladdin's Cave was filled with all manner of exotic and unusual treats to part the young people from that pocket money that was becoming fashionable at the time. Children would be at their wits' end trying to decide what to buy and at times they let fate take a hand by purchasing a wrapped surprise parcel. Beside here was the Radio Store. This was Nicky Hore's and it was the place for radiograms – the big lump of furniture with a radio and a record player cunningly concealed inside. He also sold televisions as the craze took off and had a small record selection. Looking at the amount of music on offer today it's amazing how we survived in the 1960s with a free-standing rack of LPs and the limited new releases of 6-inch singles.

In a big red-fronted shop at the corner of Keyser's Lane we had S&R Pierce, who sold hardware, seeds, guns and ammunition. Across the lane was Imco, cleaners and dyers, where you got your clothes cleaned and/or dyed in those pre-built in obsolescence days.

Although the majority of this building is in George's Street it is presented here as it shows part of Selskar Street in the late 1800s. The building on the right of the picture is the one whose rent was 'given in perpetuity to Wexford Corporation as the nucleus of a voluntary civic improvement fund' by George Bernard Shaw. (O'Connor Collection)

The relics of 'ould decency' can be seen to have existed into the 1960s and indeed well into the 1990s when we realise that the shop opposite Imco was called the L&N Tea Company – it would later move to Church Lane and remain until it changed to Super Value. What we may forget is that the full title was the London & Newcastle Tea Company, betraying its colonial origins. Next door was Dunne's Stores, where we once had Healy & Collins, famed for its overhead docket propelling system. Across from here was Ally White's, yet one more sweet shop, but this also offered ice-cream sundaes and orange sodas. They also sold a lovely spearmint bar to which my mother was semi-addicted. It had no name on the wrapper, just a sort of spiderweb design. It was here we also scoffed Macaroon bars and Flash bars.

Mayor Eddie Hall opened the new premises of RTV Rentals in 1961, on the eve of Ireland's first television station and Wexford entered the television age. In those prudent days very few people would consider buying a television; renting was the norm for your accommodation so why not do the same with the telly. OK, you never owned it but you also did not have to pay for repairs – and call-outs were a big thing in those days. Almost every other week the children sat staring out the window waiting for the 'RTV man' to come and fix the telly. The public telephone boxes would be buzzing with calls to Fergie Morris at RTV looking for a service call when the screen had gone blank, the picture kept 'rolling' or the 'thing was all snowy'.

Rochford's was another drapery shop that was popular at the time, and Donal Howlin was the assistant there. Across from here was Harry Stone's, a grocery and public house, and beside that was the Wexford Gas Consumers Company. Dunne's had started out in the building on the corner of Anne Street.

1966

In *Thom's Commercial Directory* of this year we note that twenty of the thirty-two public houses listed for Wexford Town are on the greater Main Street. All but one of the seventeen drapers listed are on Main Street and twenty-five out of forty-three grocers and provision merchants are trading on Main Street. Among the pubs that had gone or had changed hands in the half century were Des Corish's; Barnwell's; James Breen's; Eagle Bar; Eden Vale Bar; Jack Fane's; Cinema Bar; Broader's; Paddy Carey; P. Furlong; W. Gaynor; Goal Bar; Nick Murphy's; O'Keefe's; and Traver's Purcell's. Lost or changed restaurants include Bernie's Café; Granada Grill; Ita's; Love's; Mernagh's; Bessie O'Connor's; O'Toole's; The Ritz; Sinnott's and The Star. We have also lost Buckland's, Doyle's, Finnegan's and two Whelan's newsagents from Main Street. Larger conglomerates have replaced local turf accountants such as Corcoran's, as well as Finnegan's; Cullimore and Powers.

1970

Wexford Corporation heard that a 'Car Ban on the Main Street' was the only solution to traffic problems. Garda Inspector Dan Feely said, 'a fresh solution was needed'. Councillor Peter Roche pointed out, 'The one-way system is causing problems for young mothers out shopping with cars on the footpaths.' He suggested banning all parking on Main Street and thought that a 'big park on the quay' might solve the problem. As we are well aware, this did not happen.

1971

In 1971 in His and Hers Boutique at 91 South Main Street you could purchase 'Dainty Dresses in sizes 34 to 42 for £2-10-0'. A hot pants dress and matching skirt would set you back just under four quid and they also offered 'Men's Flared Slacks and gorgeous shirts with matching ties'. But the bargain of the week had to be the 'Kinky Safari Trouser Suit at 99 shillings'.

The Wexford People's Regatta in 1971 had sponsors including the Granada Grill, Woolworths, Hore's Radio Store, the *Free Press*, Fine Wool, TVRS and Cousins Mineral waters.

'Dun Mhuire Goes Discotheque' was the newspaper headline announcing the arrival of Star Trek Promotions at the parish hall with their 'lights, discs and go-go dancers'.

Strolling Main Street

'The Faythe Hessians' and the 'John Street Stone Throwers' were alternative nicknames. The football teams the Faythe Harriers or Mulgannon Harriers and the John Street Volunteers perpetuated the rivalry until recently.

The youth of the two communities divided Main Street into rival territories, Anne Street being the demarcation line, and people would not venture beyond this line on a Saturday night promenade. According to tradition, this rivalry was carried to the extent that marriage between the communities was frowned upon.

4

People

All our history is about people and here we will trace the characters and incidents that make it all so real when we look back at our heritage. A number of mayors are included here due to them also operating businesses on Main Street.

Balfe, Michael

Although born in Dublin, Michael William Balfe spent much of his youth in Wexford, where he was master of the military band while still a young man. During much of that period he resided at North Main Street, almost directly opposite what was then White's Hotel. In later years he studied under the likes of Rossini and wrote music for ballet and operas. He was the musical director and principal conductor when Jenny Lind, the 'Swedish Nightingale', made her London debut. His best-known work is *The Bohemian Girl*, featuring the song 'I Dreamt I Dwelt in Marble Halls', which has been recorded in recent times by Enya and Sinead O'Connor, among others. Balfe's 1857 opera *The Rose of Castile* brought him 'full circle' to Wexford when it was the work performed at the first Wexford Festival Opera in 1951.

Billington, James

James Billington is credited with introducing clogs to Wexford at his shop on South Main Street. He had learned his trade in Preston in Lancashire, where the footwear of wooden sole with leather uppers was popular with miners, among others. His move to Wexford was based on marriage to a girl from Mayglass in rural Wexford, who met him in the English town. They arrived in Wexford in 1911 and started manufacturing clogs in the rear of the premises that, like so many of the time, had stabling on the site. The birch and sycamore wood was sourced in rural Wexford and brought to town by horse-drawn transport. The clogs were particularly popular with Pierce workers but also attracted customers from as far away as Bray, County Wicklow.

Bridges, George

George Bridges was our quintessential harbinger of Christmas for decades. The summer excursions to Rosslare were only beginning to peter out as his little teasers began to appear in the notes sections of the local newspapers. The tag would be 'Sixteen weeks to Christmas', followed by a reminder to start planning, saving or 'putting things by'. Wexford's version of Macy's emanated not from a huge multi-storey emporium but from a little shop in Selskar that was probably no more than 10ft wide and 30ft deep, although he did have another outlet further up the street and expanded to opening a storeroom in Trimmers Lane as the fateful date approached.

George Bridges was Selskar and Christmas to many people. In a newspaper interview he recalled 200 years of Bridges' presence in that area of Wexford. His forefathers had been involved in the hire of horses, carts and sidecars from 18 Selskar Street for centuries.

The familiar Bridges shop began as a sweet shop operated by Mary Elizabeth Bridges in 1920 and sold fruit and ice cream. Her husband, Joseph, was a barber and George recounts that a regular customer was M.J. O'Connor, the solicitor, who had a regular appointment to be shaved in his own office at 8 o'clock every morning.

George began his working life as an apprentice in Lipton's. This was a grocery store that survived into the 1960s and was probably a part of a British chain of which we had quite a number in Wexford. His wages on starting amounted to 13s 7d.

It was in 1945 that he became more involved in the shop that would define him for Wexford people and he recalled travelling to the markets in Dublin seeking out new toys to enthral the boys and girls of the town. As time progressed the wholesale toy market was the domain of the bigger manufacturers and he ended up travelling to London to stock the famous Triang, Hornby and Meccano toys. In addition to these the shop was a Mecca for Matchbox and Dinky cars. These were collected, swapped, raced and treasured by generations. Many of these still no doubt grace the glass cabinets of doting grandfathers, who recall that trip to Selskar with a few bob to spend hours looking, choosing, changing their mind and eventually carrying home that little vehicle in its cardboard box. Bridges closed its doors in 1994 but the shop and the man remain vivid in the memories of Wexford and Christmas.

Byrne, Samuel

He was born in 1810, the son of John Byrne, married to Esther Fortune and later Ann Atkin, who had a brazier foundry employing more than fifty people in Foundry Lane, later Patrick's Lane. Samuel was indentured as an apprentice to watchmaker Ambrose Fortune for seven years. Fortune's shop was located at 57 North Main Street and later became Richard's.

He finished that apprenticeship on 27 October 1832 at the age of 22 and was attested as 'very clever at restaining jewellery'. He opened his own business

SOUTH MAIN STREET, WEXFORD

Healy & Collins shops dominate this picture with premises on both sides of the street at South Main Street as well as their delivery van in centre position. Also of note is M.J. (Matty) Furlong's shop and the Central Bar. Two-way motor traffic is also to be seen.

at 50 South Main Street as a master clock maker and jeweller, dying of a stroke in his store on 7 December 1858. His wife, Mary Moore Byrne, advertised in the *Wexford Independent* in 1859 that business would continue with a 'first-class workman employed'. She managed the shop for eighteen years before eventually selling it and its contents and emigrating to Canada.

Cardiff, Robert
Robert Cardiff was elected Mayor of Wexford on 3 February 1847, succeeding Shephard Jeffaries, who had been forced to resign due to poor health. Born in 1785, Dr Cardiff was surgeon to the poorhouse and also in charge of medical matters in the County Infirmary. He was also an apothecary and had his business premises at 24 North Main Street. As mayor, he was a good administrator and carried out his duties in fine style, despite the fact that he was reluctant to accept the position in the beginning. He died on 19 February 1854 and was buried in the Franciscan graveyard.

Carey, Paddy
Although Tipperary-born, Paddy Carey became an honorary Wexfordian through his public house on South Main Street, almost opposite Coffin Corner. The story is that Paddy was a man 'always on the move', whether it was serving pints, cleaning

up or listening, like most old-style publicans of the time, to the 'sob stories' of the clientele. It was common practice for him to loan 'ten bob' to someone who was stuck, being repaid at the weekend only for the money to go out to another person in trouble. A story is told that he often lost track of the 'ten bob note', wondering if it was his or another's. Sometimes that bit of help was essential in tiding over a person taking the emigrant boat to London, where it paid for the first week's digs. Family and friends always remembered such generosity, with Paddy's Menapia Bar the venue for wakes or parties, or take-away booze (a few dozen pints of Guinness) for other celebrations. The Menapia had been The Stores (a name that seems to predominate among Wexford pubs – older Stamp's Stores and now Centenary Stores) and was bought from the Buckland family, who then moved into the newsagency business and themselves became Wexford legends.

Cheap, Charlie

I doubt if we ever bothered to learn his actual name but Charlie, whom I believe may have been from Waterford, set up his stall at the back of his van every Saturday at the Bullring. It was the forerunner of the 'pound shop' and he was the equivalent of Dublin's Hector Grey. He brought to Wexford every sort of novelty, gadget, labour saver and 'notion'. He introduced us to non-stick pans, lint-removing brushes, three-in-one toys (compass/binoculars/magnifying glass) in brittle plastic, and so much more. All eagerly awaited his banter and crowds gathered to listen more often than to purchase. He had any number of catchphrases ranging from 'it's giving change that kills me' to his famous countdowns on the prices, 'not five, not even four, not three but two – yes two for two quid'.

Crosby, James Ralph

He was elected Mayor of Wexford in 1853 for his one and only term of office. A wealthy ship owner and businessman, Mr Crosby was a very strict mayor who carried out his duties in a very efficient manner. When the results of the election of the first citizen became known to the townspeople, the hooters of all the ships on the quay were sounded to celebrate the event. Very little is known about Mr Crosby, however, and information in his obituary in the *People* newspaper is equally sparse. He was, however, a devout Catholic and a very charitable man.

Ralph Crosby died in January 1862 after a short illness.

Dillon, Joe

Joe Dillon was, I believe, in the merchant navy before returning to Wexford to open what became the extremely popular Granada Grill. The premises on South Main Street at Stonebridge was one of the first of its kind in the town back in the early 1960s, with a café and slot machines on the ground floor. However, it was the upper floor that led to it becoming part of Wexford folklore. It was in the large upper room that he put on regular bingo games in aid of the Loch Garman Silver Band two or three times a week. This was in an era when bingo was taking over from the pongo games that had been very popular as Sunday afternoon fundraisers. Other halls – especially parish halls and church halls – also took on the bingo craze with special buses ferrying people all over the county on different nights of the week. Through all these games with jackpots of 'thousands' and 'sweating on one number' the lasting question over the decades has been 'are you going to Joe Dillon's tonight'.

Greene, Alderman John

Greene was first elected Mayor of Wexford in 1854 and was to serve six more terms in 1863, 1864, 1867, 1873, 1874 and 1875. He was proprietor of the *Wexford Independent* newspaper and was certainly one of the most interesting mayors in the history of the office. His name can be found on many monuments and in many places throughout the town. He will be best remembered for suggesting the introduction of interdenominational schools, which caused a spate of controversial comment in the local press. John Greene, however, was a great survivor and his strength of character can be gauged by the fact that after all the furore surrounding his mixed religious schools remarks, he was again elected mayor on a number of occasions. His long-running battles with the rival *People* newspaper were widely spoken of and his courageous outbursts won him the respect of the people of Wexford. Mayor Greene suffered a great personal loss in March 1865 when his son, Matthew Saunders Greene, died at the age of 24. Matthew was a barrister and appeared to have a great future ahead of him. Mayor Greene died on 14 April 1890, and was buried in the Franciscan graveyard.

Harpur, James

Alderman James Harpur was elected Mayor of Wexford in 1862 for his one and only term of office. Born in 1791, he was a seed merchant with a business premises in the Bullring and a nursery at Park. Alderman Harpur was a very popular and hardworking mayor, however, his involvement in public life came to an end when he was forced to retire with chronic rheumatism. His seat on the Corporation was, however, taken over by his son, John G. Harpur, who carried the family name in municipality with great distinction. It is interesting to note, too, that James Harpur's daughter, Teresa, married John Hinton, who was also Mayor of Wexford. James Harpur died in January 1869, and was buried in the Franciscan graveyard.

Harpur, Thomas

Alderman Thomas Harpur was first elected Mayor of Wexford in 1886 and was returned to office for a second time in 1887. Born in 1846, he represented St Iberius Ward and was a corn merchant with premises on South Main Street. He lived in Riversfield House, Carcur, was quite wealthy and his caring nature resulted in the building of artisans' dwellings for the less fortunate in society. Mr Harpur was a very active member of the Borough Home Rule Club and at one stage took them on an outing to Avoca. On one occasion Mr Harpur landed himself in hot water when he attended the Queen's Jubilee celebrations but, despite this, he was a very hard working and dedicated mayor. He died in St Senan's mental home in October 1926 and is buried in Crosstown cemetery.

Jeffaries, Shephard

He was first elected mayor in September 1840, the year that Wexford lost its Charter of Incorporation because of a drop in population. Born in 1774, Mayor Jeffaries shared a business with his brother at 30 North Main Street, and lived in Barntown Castle. He was a strong chairman, was greatly respected while in office and will be best remembered for his tremendous work in successfully regaining a Charter for Wexford. He also served as chairman of the council in the years between 1840 and 1846, when he regained his mayoral status on 1 December of the same year. In January 1847, Jeffaries was again elected mayor but due to bad health was forced to resign on 3 February, less than a month after he came into

This view from the Bullring looking south on North Main Street is interesting not so much for the meat hanging outside the door of Godkins but rather the 'spectacles' sign to the right indicating the premises of an optician. Such signs were common worldwide in an era before literacy had improved to allow potential customers to read shop signs. (Lawrence Collection)

office for the third and final time. He died in 1859 and is buried in Mulrankin, Bridgetown. More than 100 vehicles and a large number of horsemen are believed to have attended his funeral from his home in Barntown to Mulrankin, indicating the high esteem in which he was held.

Kenselah, Alderman James

James Kenselah (probably Kinsella) was elected Mayor of Wexford on 1 January 1848. Born in 1780, he was a wine and spirit merchant and represented St Selskar Ward on Wexford Corporation. He was also an actuary in a lending bank, which was situated in the building known today as the Ballast Office. Alderman Kenselah was a highly respected mayor and was rewarded for his dedication to duty when he was appointed president of the Court of Conscience. This is where the petty sessions were held and appears to have been in the Tholsel in the Bullring. James Kenselah died on 19 July 1862, and is buried in St Michael's graveyard.

Lowney, John

Lowney was a man of many talents but is perhaps best known in Wexford for being one of the businessmen who helped people furnish their first home, or few rooms as it was more likely in his early days. John left school at the age of 14 to assist his father, Joseph, in a furniture business in Henrietta Street. Joseph was a cabinetmaker and stories are told that young John was regularly seen delivering the finished articles on a trolley in those days before the delivery vans plied our streets. He left the bright lights of Wexford to try his luck in Enniscorthy but rather than settling there he brought back a bride, Peggy.

His other talent was music and with his brothers Joe and Tony he formed a dance band and toured the country. In the early 1950s he had a plan that might have seen him rival the Albert Reynolds's of the showband era. He bought some land at Ferrybank and was intent on building a dancehall and entertainment complex. This was four years before the present bridge opened and access would have been via Carcur and Crosstown, so this was farsighted and ambitious. At the request of no less than the bishop, who was concerned about young ladies' safety, he abandoned the idea but not the music. Instead he transferred his ambition to Redmond Hall in Spawell Road, where the husband and wife team managed a venue that sped the romantic life of young Wexford. A story is told that a regular serenade at Redmond Hall on a Sunday night was Dan Kelly singing 'Danny Boy' for the adjacent convent dwellers of St John of God.

In 1956 Lowney decided to concentrate his efforts once more on furniture and opened his first Wexford shop at 61 South Main Street. Within a few years they had acquired the adjoining premises and expanded to become the Universal Stores. That was in the late 1960s and their furniture store covered a floor area almost unheard of in a provincial town. The business grew and expanded into other areas such as electrical, televisions and everything to make a house a home. Never one to sit still, John sought other business opportunities. He opened an auction room that drew large crowds, no doubt entertained by a man well used to performance. Lowney later turned the Long Room public house that had been Wickham's Brewery in the past into a large snooker club, attracting world-class players and tournaments to Wexford. In true Wexford backhanded compliment tradition, we often forget the person although his name lived on as we referred to Lowney's Mall as if it were an ancient thoroughfare from medieval days.

McClure, Robert

This giant of international exploration was born in Wexford on 28 January 1807, the son of a naval officer. At an early age he went to Sandhurst military school in England. From there he joined the Royal Navy and served on Nelson's *Victory*. However, it is for exploration rather than fighting that this son of Wexford is best remembered. Commanding HMS *Investigator*, he discovered the Northwest Passage, allowing ships to sail around the north coast of the Americas. McClure wrote from the Arctic to his uncle, the Revd John Elgee of St Iberius's church, Wexford. Headed 'HMS Resolute Dealy Island, Barrow's Strait' in April 1853, he writes of the 'long tedious and terrible navigation of that fearful Polar Sea which has for four hundred years baffled the navies of maritime Europe'. He also states that 'the N W Passage has been discovered by Investigator, which was decided on 26 October 1850 by a sledge party over the ice'. On 26 September 1854 he wrote:

> My Dear Uncle from your affectionate nephew Robert McClure. You will be happy to hear that congratulations have poured upon me from all quarters, and the sincerest from those who know me best, my old mess-mates and captains. I ought equally to appreciate the kind sentiments which you tell me are cordially expressed by my fellow townsmen of Wexford. I am no longer in the Investigator, she was deserted in June 1853, my good friend Kellett thinking we had persevered sufficiently in an attempt to get the ship through it was a sad disappointment after the sacrifice to achieve what was the height of my ambition, the bringing home of my little barque. In June 1853 we left – (but) – it was 18th August before the Resolute got clear of her winter quarters and on the 12th Sept. was again encircled within the icy trammels of Barrow straight. In April Sir Edward Belcher determined … the ships were to be deserted and the crews to proceed to Beechey Island … arrived 26th August near Cape Osborn on the day which Phoenix made her most welcome appearance.

McClure was knighted for his efforts. He died in London in 1873.

Names

Over the centuries Main Street has lost many established businesses and the families associated with them. These included:

Holbrook; Lelly; Timpson; Ousalem (domestic servant); Kailsher (bazaar manager); Lively (bazaar assistant); Boleyn (housekeeper); Lynders; Mokely (domestic servant); Hummer; Cootey; Shudall and Cruise (grocer's assistant).

O'Connor, Michael Joseph

O'Connor was a merchant and was born in Wexford in 1835. At one stage he lived at 3 Lower George Street. He had brothers living in Wexford and sisters, while a niece was Minnie O'Connor, who built the eight red brick houses at Glena Terrace. Minnie carried on the building trade of her father and grandfather Timothy O'Connor and Patrick O'Connor. Michael Joseph O'Connor served his time as an apprentice to Patrick O'Connor, building a church at Curracloe, when he met Johanna Murphy. They lived in North Main Street, where they opened a bakery and lived above. In 1868 they extended their premises and carried on a very successful bakery business. Their children were born in the premises over the bakery and were called 'the Bakers Dozen'.

Sullivan's store on North Main Street was an excellent example of a shop making the most of its frontage. The windows were seen as the ideal advertisement for the wares on offer but the flat frontage was limited. Sullivan's, like others, decided to forego some interior space to allow for this arcade front that doubled the viewing space. (Rossiter Collection)

O'Connor, Mary

Mary O'Connor, a builder and contractor, erected Glena Terrace some time prior to 1879 for Thomas J. O'Reilly. She was also a dealer in antiques with a glass and china warehouse at 98 North Main Street. Many examples of her work may still be seen on Main Street and most are easily recognised by the 'construction in red brick with yellow brick dressings'.

O'Herron, General John

One of Napoleon's favourite generals, John O'Herron, was born at 34 North Main Street around 1796. His father, John Joseph Herron, was hanged on the old Wexford Bridge in the Insurrection of 1798. Count and Countess Sutton of Clonard, a family with strong French connections, adopted the boy as she was his aunt.

The young John Herron put an O in front of his name in France to underpin his origins and then went on to rise through the ranks to become one of Napoleon's generals before returning to Wexford in 1868. His fate in later life is lost in the mists of time, although a painting of him with Napoleon is reputed to hang in the Louvre. Incidentally, in 2005 a descendant of General John O'Herron returned to Wexford in the person of Australian Ambassador Dr John Herron. A former Australian cabinet minister, Dr Herron said that his family's origins in County Wexford dated back to the 1500s when his English-born ancestor Nicholas Herron was sent to Ireland to 'subjugate the Irish and teach them some manners'. Nicholas Herron went on to marry Cecily Moore, a daughter of Sir Thomas Moore. The modern day Herrons' links with their distinguished ancestor are recognised by the Sir Thomas Moore Society, giving our Main Street another link to international history.

Redmond, John Edward

Opposite Doyle and Nolan's stands a monument to John Edward Redmond. His youth was spent in the walled town, which was locked at nights from sunset to sunrise, and around it from the Faythe to Selskar lay a fringe of small thatched houses. Its shopping centre was from Corn Market and Back Street. The town had no thoroughfare on the waterfront. Its private ship wharves lay behind merchants' houses on Main Street and tailed off at either end into sea marshes. Main Street itself was the docks road and the citizens were jostled with packhorses laden with kegs and bales travelling to and from the wharves. The Georgian streets were being built and the embankments of the quay were under construction. Macadam was revolutionising the making of roads. Post-chaises and stagecoaches were replacing riding hacks and wheeled carts and packhorses.

Roche, Fr James

James Roche was born on South Main Street at the northern corner with Oyster Lane in 1801. The family were 'of the merchant class' and he was educated in the school of Mr Behan in George's Street before studying for the priesthood. His family business background may have assisted him in his very successful efforts in parishes after his ordination. In Ferns in 1840 he found his parish in debt and with a church half built. He managed to have the debt cleared and the church completed before being transferred to Wexford Town in 1850. Here he was instrumental in getting work started to construct not one but two churches simultaneously. On a visit to Rome in 1854 he had an audience with Pope Pius XI and received an Apostolic Blessing for 'all parishioners who made donations towards the new churches'. The churches – our Twin Churches – were completed with a few years.

Shaw, George Bernard

It is a little known fact that the writer and playwright George Bernard Shaw has a Wexford connection. While we can find no reason for it, he bequeathed the rental income from his property at Selskar (directly opposite George Street) to Wexford Corporation in 1940.

Sparrow, Francis

While we know little about Francis Sparrow, his advertisement in the *Wexford Independent* in 1841 helps us understand the size and importance of Main Street houses of that time. He advertised the premises to lease as he was retiring from business and described it as a 'large and excellent dwelling house with roomy shop', saying, 'for any line of business the situation cannot be surpassed'. The house boasted a large drawing room, parlour and eight bedrooms with a 'capital basement story [*sic*] and several houses in the rere [*sic*]'. The 'houses' probably refer to outhouses or sheds.

Stafford, James J.

James J. Stafford was born in South Main Street on 26 November 1860 to Patrick Stafford, who worked for Jasper Walsh & Company, timber merchants at The Crescent. The family also had a small grocery store at South Main Street. James was educated at the Christian Brothers and his first employment was at the Wexford Dockyard, where he rose to managerial rank. In 1891 he purchased his first ships, the schooner *Mary and Gertrude* and the ketch *Zion Hill*, and continued to add to his fleet. In 1900 he went into the coal business, having purchased the premises of John E. Barry on Paul Quay.

He was to add furniture, hardware, funeral undertaking, a public house, electricity generation and more to the empire over the years that followed. In 1915 he bought a guesthouse in Trinity Street and expanded into an adjoining premises as the Talbot Hotel. In 1918 he purchased the Wexford Timber Company that had existed in various guises at The Crescent since 1817. By 1928 he had a confectionary company producing jams and sweets as Golden Crescent.

In 1931 he had three companies: J.J. Stafford & Company, Wexford Timber Company and Wexford Steamship Company. He was also chairman of Irish Motor Ships Limited and Messrs P. Donnelly & Company of Dublin. He was involved in the Talbot Hotel and the Talbot Garage, and it is said that he was the first petrol stockist in Wexford.

In addition to the many business pursuits, he was Mayor of Wexford for three full terms at a time when being mayor was more than ceremonial. It also included the duty of chief magistrate and one that was well placed for 'controlling the import and export trade'. In 1928 Stafford's premises on the quay stretched from Trinity Street to the north side of Crescent Quay. On Main Street they went from King Street to Oyster Lane on the east side and a wide block on the west side reached back to The Boker, or Joseph's Street.

For us growing up in Wexford of the 1950s our contacts with Stafford's were mainly through going to Paul Quay to order coal, which would be delivered by a grey lorry and the sacks carried in by Tom Cleary. We also watched out for any rare appearances in their 'box' in the Capitol Cinema, but I cannot ever recall seeing them there.

Swift, Tommy

Although he did not have a shop on Main Street, Tommy Swift was one of its best-known merchants. Tommy was a small man with a huge voice. He wheeled a small makeshift 'wooden pram' and could raise the crows with his shouts of 'Herald a Press' as he sold his newspapers outside the Capitol Cinema. The *Evening Herald* and the *Evening Press* were both published in Dublin each weekday from early afternoon. Tommy would hawk his copies to the crowds queuing for the pictures each evening. Anyone recalling those newspapers will remember one or two columns on the bottom of the front page where 'late breaking news' was superimposed at some stage between the printed articles leaving Dublin and landing in our hands.

Walsh, John, JP

He was first elected Mayor of Wexford in 1852. Born in 1788, he was an auctioneer and had a business at Crescent Quay and 3 North Main Street.

He was very deeply interested in improving the town and will be best remembered for his efforts to provide the inhabitants with piped water. He was very strong on the need for proper roads and footpaths and never missed an opportunity to express his opinion. John Walsh was re-elected mayor in 1859, and again in 1865, when he was 77 years old. He died in 1868 at the ripe old age of 80, just a short few months before his son, John Joseph Walsh, was elected to the same high office. Mr Walsh Senior, one of the town's finest mayors, was buried in the Franciscan graveyard in the family mausoleum. He was the oldest mayor since the Charter of Queen Victoria and possibly the most senior in the history of the office. Another striking feature was his physical stature and people frequently stopped to stare at this very tall, fine-looking man.

Walsh, Alderman Richard

He was first elected Mayor of Wexford in 1849 and was returned to office in 1850 following the death of John Cooney. Born in 1791, he was a general merchant with a business on the corner of Henrietta Street and Main Street.

Alderman Walsh was very successful in his business life and at the time of his death he was quite wealthy. A highly intelligent man, he was deeply interested in the plight of the poor and often challenged the well-off members of the community to help their less fortunate townsfolk. He represented St Iberius Ward on the council for many years until he died on 8 August 1867. He was buried in the Franciscan graveyard.

The only remaining memorial to this fine gentleman is a stained-glass window in the Church of the Immaculate Conception.

Willis, Thomas

Thomas Willis is another name from the past on Wexford Main Street and, although we cannot establish an address for him, he gives us another insight into trade on the street. In February 1857 he took out an advertisement in the *Wexford Independent*

This ingenious little advertising piece was designed to fit into the lid of a pocket watch. (Rossiter Collection)

advising 'his Numerous Friends and the public' that he intended to retire from business in favour of his grandson Edwin Willis and his foreman James Codd as he was 'getting rather old and infirm'. He notes, 'on particular occasions he will give them assistance'. He ends the advertisement in a very businesslike manner, 'T.W. also expects that those who are indebted to him will on or before 25 March pay up in order that the accounts of the Establishment may not be confused.'

Voters

In December 1844 the *Wexford Conservative* printed a list of those who had applied for the right to vote in an upcoming election based on their rights as of that time as freemen or on rateable valuation. Among those listed for Main Street we find:

Francis Brown – shopkeeper – freeman
Michael Cahill - poulterer – dwellinghouse situated on Main Street – £10
William Chambers - saddler – dwellinghouse situated on Main Street – £10
John Corry – shopkeeper – dwelling house situated on Main Street – £10
Nicholas Downey - shopkeeper – dwellinghouse situated on Main Street – £10
James Grace - shopkeeper – dwellinghouse situated on Main Street – £10
Thomas Jeffries - shopkeeper – dwellinghouse situated on Main Street – £10
William Keating - shopkeeper – dwellinghouse situated on Main Street – £10
Martin Murphy - shopkeeper – dwellinghouse situated on Main Street – £10
Michael Murray – ships carpenter – dwellinghouse situated on Main Street – £10
Mathew Parle – brazier – dwellinghouse situated on Main Street – £10
Michael Reck – coach maker - dwellinghouse situated on Main Street – £10
James Ward Richards – apothecary - dwellinghouse situated on Main Street – £10
James Rowan – flour seller - dwellinghouse situated on Main Street – £10
Robert Stafford - shopkeeper – dwellinghouse situated on Main Street – freeman
James Sinnott – baker - dwellinghouse situated on Main Street – £10
Richard Sinnott - shopkeeper – dwellinghouse situated on Main Street – freeman
Patrick Whitty - shopkeeper – dwellinghouse situated on Main Street – £10
John Wickham – merchant - dwellinghouse situated on Main Street – £10

5

What Was Where

—ɱ—

It is always fascinating to look back on previous businesses that operated on Main Street. To assist you in your own research we attach here as comprehensive a list of the buildings, including as many former businesses as we can locate, going back over the decades and centuries. Like most towns, the number system may have altered slightly over time. This is most obvious because for the most part odd numbers are on the side away from the harbour on North Main Street but the process is reversed on South Main Street. To add to the confusion, a few buildings at Stonebridge now have even numbers although they are located on the harbour side (marked ★).

The listings are derived from a number of sources as listed in the bibliography and dated where possible. Unfortunately some businesses may be missed if they were only current at times between the business directories and advertisements available.

Where dates are included in brackets it denotes a year the business was advertised in a publication.

The entries in **BOLD** refer to the situation in June 2017.

North Main Street

1   **Peter Mark** – hairdresser; People Newspapers; Home & Colonial Stores; Stamp – ironmonger and gunpowder office (1858). The building concealed the entrance to Archer's Lane, which stretched from Main Street to High Street and in the late 1900s the remnants of the 'stepped' lane could still be walked in going from the office of *People* newspapers to the 'works'.

2   **Sherwood** – chemist; Pat Lambert – baker/auctioneer; J. Lambert – coal merchant.

3   **CEX** – electrical store; Sony Shop – electrical; Joyce's – china shop; Brian O'Connor – shoes; Peter Hanton – glassware; Peter Hanton – bookseller, stationery and coach office (advertised

This is the 2017 exterior of 59 South Main Street.

'cheap stationery'; playing cards 2s in 1884); Esmonde's – town house.

4   **Claire's** – accessories; Boston – clothes; Book Station – books / stationery; Tabi – clothes; Benetton – clothes: Bessie O'Connor's – café; Alicia & Jane Dixon – drapery and millinery.

5   **ERSK** – clothes; Blue Mountain – clothes; Cadogan's – bookies; Corcoran – bookmaker; Stewart – confectionery; Patrick Holbrook – barber and tobacconist, 'Tonsorial Parlour for shaving and hair cutting'; Mgt. Holbrook – hairdresser/perfumer; Kehoe & O'Sullivan – insurance (1914).

6   **Dillon's** – watches and jewellery; Spectra – Photo Shop; Whelan's – barber (first public baths in Wexford); Mrs Pierce – apothecary; Richard's – apothecary.

7 **Gerard's** – clothes; Token – boutique; Book Centre; Fortes – café; Joyce's – hardware; McIlroy's Tip Top Shop – stationery; McGoldrick – butcher.

8 **McCauley** – chemist; Sinnott – chemist; J.F. Kehoe – footwear; Patrick Joyce – draper.

9 **Hassett's (Brian > Tom > Ned)** – chemist; Myles Doyle – stationers/books/general (1910).

10 **Donna Anna** – clothes; Metro – clothes; Fox – sweets (hairdressers upstairs); Lavelle – draper; Sutton – fruit and restaurant 'home and foreign fruiterer' (1909); James Walsh – fruit.

11 *as 9*

12 Pamela **Scott** – clothes; Michael H – clothes; Doyle Lowney – solicitors; Ted Doyle – solicitor; Rochford's – pub (Irish House).

13 **Industry** – clothes; Corry's – draper; Manchester and Scotch House – advertising 'specialists in black costumes for every occasion'.

14 **Sasha** – clothes; Kelly – carpets; Hipps – menswear; Kerr's – jewellers (upstairs); William Rossiter – nursery/seeds/hardware (advertised as an agricultural implement factory and general ironmongery warehouse in 1872).

15 **Industry** – clothes; Corry's – drapery; Kehoe – auctioneer; Kehoe – menswear; Peter Cassin (1876) – printing.

16 **Cullen's (closed)** – children's wear; J.F. Kehoe drapery (1869); Ned Foley – 'high class' grocery; John Fitzsimon – drapery and millinery; Nunns – town house.

17 **Carphone Warehouse** – phone shop; Hynes – jeweller; Joyce's – ladies' wear; Joyce's – fancy goods; O'Keefe – sweets.

18 **New Look** – clothes; Kelly – bakers (1910); Harris – butcher; O'Reilly – draper; William Busher – bacon etc (1888).

19 **Hynes** (closed) – jeweller; Cards & Things; Cullimore – butchers; Murphy – greengrocer; Moran – café; Kirwan – butcher; J. Corish – draper.

20 **Lifestyle Sports** – sportswear; M and J – restaurant; Wheelers – shoes; Gilbey – wine merchants; Leverette and Frye – grocery/Italian warehousemen/'By Royal Appointment'; in 1858 Rebecca Hughes advertised that she was moving her drapery business to this address (saying it was beside the *People* newspaper); A.W. & F. Hughes advertised 'supplies for Lent' in 1873, including Shetland and Norway cod and bloaters.

21 **Euro Savers** – discount store; Adams – children's wear; Saxone – shoes; Burtons – clothes; Harpur – hardware; Harpurs – carpets; Kelly – drapery (1903).

22   **Westgate Design** – various; Nangle's – restaurant; Kavanagh's
      – bakery 'finest quality plain and fancy bread' (1910); B. Williams –
      draper; Leverette & Frye.

23   *as 21*

24   **Natural Health Store** – health foods; SIPTU – trade union office;
      Corish Hall; Mrs Walsh – typing school; National Forester Hall;
      Technical School; Dr Creane's house.

25   **Cappuccinos** – café; Wooden Brassiere – café; Breen's – drapery;
      Walsh – drapery.

26   **Euro Giant** – discount store; Tower Bar; Oak Lounge; T. Banville
      – grocery/bar (1962); Pat Whelan – grocery/bar; William Scallan –
      tea/sugar/wines/'foreign spirits'.

27   **Meteor** – phone store; Hairdresser; Donna Anna – clothes; J. Ffrench
      – grocery; Cosgrave's – grocery; Armstrong – grocery; Miss Breen
      – hats; London & Newcastle – grocery; D.J. Healy – hardware and
      cycle agent – also 2 Rowe Street (1891).

28   **Hug Me** – phone store; Three – phone store; Pizza Factory; Doyle's
      – butchers; Fortune's – butchers; Harpur – hardware storage; Harpur
      – carpets; Mrs M. Joyce – china and glass (advertised as opposite
      Rowe Street) 1877; Howard Rowe – residence.

29   **Nellie's Sweet Shop** – sweets; Jenkins – department stores; Celtic
      Laundry Depot; Singer Sewing Machines; W. Gainfort's – draper/
      books/news.

This building at Stonebridge South Main Street shows the trademark brickwork that denoted so many buildings erected by Mary O'Connor, building contractor, in the early 1900s. (Rossiter Collection)

30   **AIB** – bank; Munster & Leinster (December 1923) – bank; Henry
        Dempsey – provisions; Jeffare's – chandlers; Jeffare's Bros – grocery/
        tea/wines/spirits warehouse & bonding store (est. 1818).

31   **Wexford Bookshop & Shu 4 U** – book store and shoe store;
        Jenkins; T. Williamson – drapery; R. Young – drapery and footwear,
        'men's nailed boots 9/6 & girls glace kid boots 8/6 repairs done
        cheaply', 'If you are a big man get a big shirt' (1917); William
        Timpson – clocks/jewellery; Emigration Agent, land and insurance
        agent (supplied Rowe Street church clock).

32   **AIB** – bank; Edenvale – public house (Jackie Culleton owner with
        dental practice upstairs); Walsh – public house; O'Connor & Parker –
        public house.

33   **McKeons** – shoes; Jenkins; Byrne – draper; P. Carty – draper; W.B.
        Lee – linen and woollen draper (1877).

34   **Sports Shop** – sportswear; Goggin's – hardware; Fennell's –
        drapery; Mernagh's – café; Robinson's – confectionery (established
        1855 by Mary Robinson, late manager of Shelbourne Hotel, Dublin,
        'at the embodiment [*sic*] of the Wexford Regiment).

35   **Neville's Entry** – door to lane.

36   **Sports Shop** – sportswear; Goggin's – hardware; Fennel's – drapery;
        Mernagh's – café (Kehoe & O'Sullivan insurance brokers advertised
        for here); Empire Cigar Divan; John Hagarty – church furniture sale
        was advertised in 1859 offering items 'from the continent' including
        gongs, figures (Saints Patrick and Joseph included), lamps, etc.

37   **Phone King** – phone accessories; Health Food Store; Tile Centre;
        Jenkins; Beauty Store; Sandra – drapery; Traynor's – hardware;
        Lipton's – grocery.

38   **Mace** – convenience store; Centra – convenience store; Tack Room
        – pub; Tommy Roche's – pub; Jack Fanes – pub and grocery; Luke
        Cowman – pub and grocery; Thomas Martin's – grocery and spirits
        (1876); an art auction was held at Mrs Hughes' house of this address
        in 1858.

39   **Vodafone** – phone store; Quigley – children's wear; Quigley –
        sportswear; P.J. O'Connor – hardware; Healy's – ladies exclusive
        drapery.

40   **Stone's** – solicitors; National Irish Bank; Northern Bank; Traynor's
        – hardware (to 1976); Somers & Porter – provisions store; Tholsel.

41   **O'Brien's Sandwich Bar**; Target Pound Shop; O'Connor – gift
        and china shop; Kevin Moran's – children's clothes; Madame Gaul –
        ladies' outfitters.

43   **Three** – phone store; Roche – knitwear; Bank of Ireland - Money Exchange; Smart Waves; Kirby's Pharmacy; R.H. Cooper – 'surgeon/ mechanical dentist'; Cooper & Boyle – dentists (1914); Cooper's Medical Hall advertised Laurence' Hair Dye – blonde to raven black at 1*s* to 3/6 per bottle.

44   **William Fortune** – stationery, novels, toys, carpets, briar pipes and views of Wexford – in 1855 advertised 'Cheap Sale – Britannia Metal Teapots 10*s*'.

45   **Evolution** – clothes; ACC – bank; Sullivan's – drapery; McHugh & Druhan – drapery; Corporation Wages Office (upstairs); Tyler's Shoes; The Arcade; W. McLaughlin – drapery and millinery.

47   **Joanne's** – café; Godkin's – bakery store; Anne Coughlin – draper and milliner.

48   **Diana Donnelly** – clothes; J. Lambert – grocery/pub; Church of Ireland rectory.

49   **Gossip** – clothes; Entry to Cornmarket centre; Godkins – provisions; McHugh and Druhan (1939) – clothing; Vizers – house paint and room paper warehouse (nearly opposite White's 1873).

51   **Uptown Girl** – clothes; Sarah Godkin – bakers/flour dealers; Col. Tottenham of Taghmon – town house.

52   **Fat Face** – clothing; First National – building society; Ritz Café; O'Brien Bookmaker; John Daly – bakers and provisions.

53   **Hamilton's** - fancy goods; Hamilton's – greengrocer; Hamilton's – hardware; Godkin's – bakery; Francis Cosgrove – baker.

54   **Boot's** – chemist; Greenacres – food hall; Frank O'Connor's – food hall; Frank O'Connor's – bakers/flour dealers (est. 1860); G.B. Cooke – gunsmith; John Wheelock – gunsmith.

56   **Crabtree** – clothes shop; Cookes – jewellers; Ambrose Fortune – watches and jewellery (1884).

57   **Ryan's** – opticians; Whitty – jeweller; Rudd – jeweller; T.H. Richards – jewellers (advertising the Emerald Isle Watch in 1909).

58   **Si Jolie** – clothes; Heritage Crystal; Dermot Hall – newsagent; John L. Doyle – stationer.

59   **Shoe Style** – footwear; O'Leary – auctioneer; Sloan's – drapery; Hynes – drapery 'suits made in three days, tweeds, serges and worsteds for 30*s* to 70*s* guaranteed made in Wexford by expert local tailors'.

60   **Ava** – clothes; Bubbles – baby wear; Options – boutique; Billy Rackard – Furniture 'cash or deferred payments' (1962); Ted Sutton – menswear; O'Reilly – drapery; Roche Brothers – drapers (1922).

This beautiful shopfront with its timberwork and sign painting is a striking example of how most Wexford shops presented to the public before the plastic and aluminium of the twentieth century. (O'Connor Collection)

61	**Irish Permanent** (closed) – building society; New Ireland Insurance; L. Faris - tea/wine/spirits; J. Kelly – tea/spirits; Redmond's Bank; in 1858 David Faris advertised 'October Brewing of Allsop's Pale and Strong Burton Ales'.
62	**Shaw's** – department store (1976); Hadden's – department store; Quinn – dentist; Brennan – dentist; W. & G. Hadden – drapery.
63	**Macken's** – pub; JP Keating – pub; Cape of Good Hope (home of 13 Club).
64	**Shaw's**; Haddens.
65–67	PW Dwyer – draper (1884).
66	**Shaw's**; Hadden's; Catherine Wetherald – grocery/wine/spirits.
68	**Shaw's**; O'Neill – sweets; Roche – sweets; Reville's – sweets; (built over exit from Roman Lane); Fardy's – leather shop.
69	**Sarah King** – clothes; General Accident – insurance; Radio Vision – TV store; Whelan's – ladies' wear; O'Connor/Coughlin – drapers.
70	**Murphy's Chemists**; James O'Leary – baker; Mary Cahill – drapery (1914).
71	**Corcoran's** – menswear; Whelan's – ladies wear; Daly's – salt store.
72	**Esse** – clothes; Franchesca – fabrics; TV Service Centre; Furlongs – pub; Richard Furlong – grocery/spirits (1909); M. Cahill – general merchant; Joseph Lacy – grocery and 'posting establishment', also 'mourning coaches'.
73	**Benneton** – clothes; TSB – bank; Loves Café; Eliza Gainfort – boot maker.
74	**Sa Ria** – clothes; Factory Outlet – fashions; ESB office; Stafford – glassware; Considine – draper; John Ryan – draper.
75	**Empress** – clothes; Crabtree – clothes; Jodi – ladies wear; F. Newton – jewellers; Sheila Cooke – gunsmiths.
76	**Babushka** – children's clothes; Slaney Flowers; Walkers.
77	**James Kehoe** – radio dealer; Hairdresser; Cooke's Sporting Depot (1939), guns etc. 77 North Main Street; O'Meara's – boots (1914).
78	**Rainbow** – natural food shop; Walkers.
79	**Shelley's** – café; O'Neill (Ita's) – bakery (1960); Lennon – haberdashery; Mgt. Cahill - draper/milliner (selling lawns, linens, lustres and alapacas in 1862).
80	**La Cuisine** – food; Walkers.
81	**Vodafone** – phone shop; O'Brien – drapery; John Hayes – grocer (1855 advertised Shetland ling and Labrador herring for sale).
82	**Fortunes** – chemist (1962); Healy's – cycles and hardware; R. Mayne – motor and cycle agent and cycle repairer (1902); Paul J.

Carroll – 'ready-made clothes' (advertised as 'next door to Walkers' 1884).

83   **Holland & Barrett** – health foods; Laurence Woods – jewellers; TVRS (Tom O'Rourke) – records; McMurrough's – drapery; P.J. Walsh – draper; Thomas & Nick Murphy – drapery (1914 advertised as 'formerly Stafford's'); James Stafford – draper.

84   **Empty**; Del – cleaners; Codds – flower boutique; N. Murphy – tobacconists; Moran – tobacconists; Sampson – butchers.

85   **Superdrug** - pharmacy; WexWorld – furniture; Cristelle's – fashions; Loch Garman Co-Op – hardware, seeds, oil; Auctioneer; Hannan – furniture, cycles; Rd. Shaw – furniture/cabinets (early 1800s) advertised as the 'oldest house in furniture trade in Wexford' with a tag 'every furniture from a cottage to a mansion'.

86   **Empty**; Computers; Roche – knitwear; Murphy – tobacconist, newsagent, stationery and sweets (1962); Ellen Codd – millinery; Mary & Alice Walsh – fruit.

88   **Divas & Dudes** – hairdressers; Café; Gullwell – fruit; Daniel Murphy – tailor (1910).

89   **Little Piggies** – shoes; Bag Shop; Cards Galore; Doyle – hardware; Des Corish – sweets; J. Annesley – druggist and ironmonger (Hadden's Medical Hall) 1902; Hadden's – medical hall (offered 'crystal spectacles' as well as in a sealed envelope for three shillings *Manhood*, a book dealing with 'cause of premature decline and excessive indulgence, solitary habits and infection' in 1884); Richard Webb – medical hall (pre-1830),

90   **Chan's** – Chinese restaurant; Bernie's Café (1960s); Kane's – rabbits and fowl; M.J. Smith – millinery; Murphy – seeds.

91   **Oxfam**; Wilson – greengrocers; T. Cullen – meal shop, 'the best house for oil cakes, calf feeding, flour, meal and bran' (1909); Suttons – meal shop.

93   **Sheridan** – insurance; Macken Travel; Mulligan's – newsagents; Eagle Bar; Nolan's Eagle Tea House (1910).

92   **Murphy** – cycles/fishing; Fitzpatrick – stationery and tobacco; Paris House – ladies' fashion.

93   **Sheridan** - insurance; Mackin – travel agents; Mulligan – newsagents and souvenirs; Cathy Roche – pub (Eagle Bar); M. Nolan's Eagle Tea Rooms – tea (1910); Father Kavanagh, the historian who unveiled the Pikeman statue, was born here.

94   **Empty**; Michael's – restaurant; W. Gulwell – sweets & fruit; Fitzpatrick's (1939) – 'ladies only admitted to view new stock of handbags'.

This set of photographs taken in the early twenty-first century show what the interior of many of Main Street homes would have looked like before conversion to retail and office use. (Rossiter Collection)

95	**Sheridan** – insurance; Quigley's – electrical; Mrs Sinnott – drapery (advertised in 1922 that she had reopened her shop after the holidays).
96	**Abracababra** – restaurant; Whelan's – newsagents/wallpapers; Newman's – newsagent and 'fancies'; *Wexford Independent* (established in 1769 as the *Wexford Journal*).
97	**Butlers** – post office and shop; Office City; The Bailey Café; O'Rourke's – butchers (1962); G. Lymbery – saddler and coach building (1891).
98	**Kavanagh** – tiles; Lombard & Ulster – finance; Mary (Minnie) O'Connor – china/glass/Delph; in 1858 a premises 'next to the Independent offices' was advertised with thirteen apartments (rooms), WC, yard and stable for eleven horses. It had a rear exit beside the courthouse on the quay; Colour Sergeant John Willis of the Wexford Regiment lived here until his death aged 45 in 1859 (he had served in India in earlier years).
99	**Ulster Bank**; Matt Kehoe – butcher; L. Murphy; Miss Shanahan's School for Girls.
100	**Mackin Travel** – travel agents; NRB; W. Rackard – menswear; fruit shop.
101	**Ulster Bank**; Ml. O'Connor – bacon/ham/gams/fish – advertised 1902 as 'purchasing pigs' (1962); Lyons Brother – pianoforte and harmonium warehouse (offered a second-hand Rosewood Cottage Pianoforte that cost £40 four years earlier for £30 for immediate purchase in 1872).
103/105/ 107	**Closed**; La Speranza – bar; Harpers – bar; White's Hotel (1797); Wheelock's Hotel; Miss Shanahan's School for Girls; O'Leary – hairdresser (at 103 in 1914 'patronised by clergy and gentry').
109	**Vine** – Thai restaurant; YMCA (1858).
111	**Darcy's** – clothes; Route 1 – jeans; O'Neill – electrical; O'Mahoney – hairdresser; O'Leary – hairdresser; Carty – hairdresser advertised in 1939 – 'Having added to our staff an extra ladies hairdresser, French, we are enabled to execute all orders for hair work. Hairdressing, face and scalp massaging. Save your combings and have them made up, tails, fringes, pads and curls. Member of the Incorporated Guild of Hairdressers and Wigmakers.'
113	**Hynes** – jewellers; Xtra Vision – video rentals; Mulcahy – post office; Malone's – post office.
115	**Wexford Silver** – jewellery; Ferrycarrig Crystal; Gaynors – shoes; George Taylor – auctioneer.

South Main Street

DV8 – clothes; A-wear – clothes; Joyce's – hardware, electrical etc.; Lennon & Browne – draper and milliner; National Bank; James Stamp – hardware and carpets.

Adding to the confusion of Main Street in some legal documents, this is stated to be number 1 South Main Street but in fact odd numbers are all located on the opposite side.

1   **Shoe Zone** – shoes; Tyler's – shoes; Dunne's – drapery; Lamb House (Con Collins) drapery; Lamb House (Donovan's) – drapery '2,000 pairs army boots for sale' (1917); Joseph Dalton draper; Laurence Devereux – draper; James Pettigrew lived here in 1859 (the death of his 13-year-old son John Joseph saw the child noted as 'giving great indication of talent in various ways'); Belton – drapers (1841).

2   **Pandora** – jewellery; Dynasty – jewellery; Celtic Laundry Depot; Vogue (Mrs Bond) – boutique; Furlong – saddlery; Rita Cuddihy – hairdresser (probably second floor).

3   **Carrig Donn** – clothes; Wexford Gas Consumers Company showrooms; Boggan Bros – music shop and bus service; Ailish Owens – hairdresser (upstairs 1960s).

4/6/8   **Selected** – clothes; O'Neill's – sweets; Roche – greengrocer; Bob (Sutton) Doyle – vegetables; Taylor's – newspaper owner; Charlie Vize – 'high class photographer' (upstairs 1909); Hassett's – developing.

5   **Book Centre** – books; Stones – grocery/pub; Kehoe & O'Sullivan Insurance Agents (1910); W. Devereux – grocery/wine/spirits; in 1832 A. Prince advertised set up as an optician at Devereux's.

7   **O'Neill's** – sweets; Marlowe's – cleaners; Healy & Collins – drapery; Nolan – pub; Blake – pub; Keatings – teas/stout/malt/grocery – 'also owned The Cape at this time' (1910); Thomas Harpur – malt/corn/coal/culm also maltsters and ship owner; Gaelic League Hall.

9/11   **Dunne's** (closed) – drapery; Healy and Collins – drapery; Gaelic League Hall; Brien and Keating – ironmonger/plumber/cabinets (1910).

10/12   **Villa** – clothes; Barrat – shoes; Ffrench – curtains; Howlin – drapery; Rochford – drapery 'gents summer suitings' (1914); McClean – painter and decorator.

13   **Dunne's** (closed) – drapery; O'Rourke – butcher.

14   **Game Stop** – computer games; Martins – jewellers; Frances Monahan – 'Wexford's leading gift store (1962); Hanrahan –

With the advent of piped water and sewerage the family homes on Main Street converted to using flush toilets. In many cases an interior room was subdivided for use as the bathroom, but not in all cases. This is an example of how an 'outside toilet' was 'hung' on to an upper floor of a house with a door broken through from one of the existing rooms. (Rossiter Collection)

stationery, paper bag factory, print works, hats; Brien and Keating – hardware, carpets, 'bell hanging', 'lock making'.

15 **Dunne's** (closed) – drapery; Healy & Collins; Nolan – drapery; Joseph Murphy – chandler, hardware, guns, beds, paint, gas mantles and globes, cartridges, blasting powder and fuses 'all goods sold at the lowest cash prices' (1909).

16 **Name It** – clothes; Paddy Doyle – butcher; D. Cullimore – butcher; M.J. Furlong – books/stationery/music instruments ('Furlong's your man') offering American organ for sale in 1884 for £9 (1962); Thomas Devereux – hardware and cutlery (in 1859 he advertised that he had taken over his grandfather William Trigg's brush factory with 'all kinds of brushes made to order').

17 **Pound City**; McManus – shoes; L&N – grocery (1962); William Devereux – grocery and pub.

18/20 **JD Sports** – sportswear; RTV – television rental (later electrical goods sales); Healy & Collins – drapery.

19 **Rob's Ranch House** – restaurant; Robertino's – café; Nunn's – corn office; W. Murphy – jeweller and travel agent; William Timpson – jeweller 'agent for passenger steamers to the colonies and all parts of America – established 1792' (1909); E. & J. O'Connor (late of Todd Burns & Co.) – silks, mantles, parasols, straw bonnets & feathers (1859).

21 **Charlie Pierce** – menswear; Fisher – ice-cream parlour – fish and chips (first in Wexford).

22 **Tabi** – clothes; Four Seasons – china; Dick Trappe – fabrics; Alex (Allie) White's – sweets and ice cream; Henrietta Byrne – drapery and millinery warerooms [*sic*] (1891).

23 **Charley's** – ladies wear; Arthur Kelly – electrical; N. Hore – toys and radio; Curran & Wall – drapery; Lambert – drapery (1914), in 1917 'first spring show of 1917 goods, millinery and mantles'.

24 **Eir** – phone shop; Herterich – pork butcher (1962); Whitty – sweets; The Bon (Shanley) – ice cream; George Holmes – jeweller; J.T. Holmes – draper.

25 **Specsavers** – opticians; Commodore – pub; Hore's – Radio House – electrical, records etc.; Cousins & Co. – grocers, wine and spirit merchants (1885); Peter Fardy – grocery and spirits (1857); John Cullen – grocery and spirits.

26 **Rattigans** – jeweller (1962); Underwood – hardware/coffin maker/ cycle repair. Advert in 1939, 'pram wheels re-tyred'; Laurence Codd – seed dressing.

27   **Penney's** – drapery; Woolhead's – toys; Connicks – grocer (1891).

28   **Fehily's** – chemists (1962); Fitzpatrick Model Pharmacy; A. Murphy
        – bonnets (1903); Christina Joyce – drapery.

29   **Penney's** – drapery; Woolworths; Frank Gaul – hardware and
        undertaker; Sinnott's – hardware selling 'patent WCs' in 1859 (owned
        Theatre Royal); Sinnott's, 29 South Main St tickets for Theatre Royal
        1939; site of Kenny's Hall.

30   **Rebel & Rock** – hairdressers; White's – records; Imco – cleaners;
        Toomey's – second-hand library; Donnelly – foundry; P.J. Carroll –
        music teacher.

31   **Hore's Stores**; Bucklands – newsagents; Philips – Bread shop, 'Listen
        to me, for health sake only eat Phillips's' (1909); *People* – newspaper.

32/34   **Fitzgerald's** – clothing; S. & R. Pierce – hardware and seeds;
        Connicks – fruit shop; Connicks – draper (oil coats for sailors and
        farmers).

35   **Breda's** – clothes; The Orchard – fruit; Kerwood – butchers.

36/38   **Barker's** – gifts; Barkers – china and travel agent (motor car hire);
        Barker – Marine Stores (est. 1843).

37   **Simon Lambert & Sons** – public house; Simon's Place – pub;
        Dillon – pub; Kate Codd – grocer; E. Hayes & Co. – boots and shoes,
        'They are made on our own premises by skilled workmen' (1891).

39/41   **Mountain Warehouse** – outdoor clothing; Wool Shop; Miss
        Dempsey – tea rooms; Dempsey – Delph and second-hand books
        and comics; Temperance Hotel (upstairs).

40   **Barkers** – gifts; Paddy Lyons – shoes (1962); Tyler's – boot/shoes.

42   **Panache** – clothes; Geoghan – jewellers; B.J. Kerr's – jewellers; Louis
        Kerr – jeweller (1962); S. Sinnott – jeweller and optician.

43   **Megamix** – novelties; W. Jeffery – travel agent.

44   **Boutique Bliss** – clothes; The Union – boutique; B.J. Kerr's –
        jewellers; Murphy & Roche – painters and decorators (1960s);
        Cranitch – stationery; Morris – handmade boots, 'Encourage home
        trade and wear Morris's Wexford Made Boots' (1910).

46   **Trespass** – clothes; Nolan's – café; Mamie Scallan – furniture; John
        Hoare – saddler/harness maker; Mary Codd – church organist and
        music teacher.

47   **Itech** – accessories; Taxi office; David Cadogan – electrical.

48   **Vape** – e-cigarettes; Singer – sewing machines; Sullivan's Bargain
        Stores; Francis Sparrow – Wexford brass and iron foundry (1841).

49   **Sheridan** – photography; Bookends – second-hand books; Power –
        bookmakers.

50	**Candy** – clothes; Paper Chain – cards; Bucklands – newsagents, pipes, cigars and pouches 'large well selected stock of 6*d* novels'; Gordon & Furlong – plumbers; Daniel Carroll – pawn broker and tobacconist; J.J. Kelly – cigar importer/auctioneer with auction yard at The Old Pound; Samuel Byrne – clocks and watches (in 1859 Mrs Byrne advertised that following the death of her husband, Samuel, she had employed a 'first rate workman' to continue the business).
51	**Costa** – coffee shop; South 51 – pub; Tim's Tavern – pub; Eddie Hall – pub; Hannan – pub; Codd – grocery and spirits; Pat Heffernan – general merchant.
50a	**Regency Gold** – jewellers; Hynes – butcher.
52	**Dealz** – discount store; Panache – ladies' wear; Wallace – tailor.
53	**Uncle Sam's** – fast food; Peter Murphy – grocery; Heffernan – grocery; J. Bucklet – draper.
54	**Dealz** – discount store; Computer World; Beauty Shop; Crabtree – clothes; Wallace's – tailors; Maggie Sheil – bread, 'Cheapest house in the trade' (1909); James Browne – bakery/meal/flour/bran.
55	**Chic Shop** (closed) – clothes/shoes; Panache – ladies' wear; Kevin Moran – drapery; Moses Harpur – pub.
56/58	**Heaton's** – department store; Coffey's (1896) – department store 'Prices bordering on the ridiculous – cottage piano £16-10-0'; Tennant's – pawnbrokers; Buckley – draper; E. Hayes Wexford – boot and shoe shop (1888); J. Buckley (1876) 58 South Main Street – hat and cap warehouse.
57	**Louaine** – boutique; Ironside – photography; Nick Murphy – pub; Cinema Bar (1960s); Teresa Stafford – grocery and spirits; Moses Harpur – public house and grocery, 'Guinness Extra Stout (Brown Label guaranteed) Bass's Ale in bottles (1909).
59	**Empty**; O'Leary – travel agent; Chic Shop – clothes; *Free Press* – newspaper; GPO – in 1892; Hayes Brothers – family grocers (1869).
60	**Heaton's** – department store; Coffey – department store; Coad – footwear; Martin Harvey – boot maker; Glasgow House – boots in 1881, advertised 'no slop goods kept'.
61/63	**Lowney's Mall** (closed); Lowney – Universal stores; Hearne – drapery; Joseph O'Connor – bakery; Howard Rowe – bakery; Godkin's Stores.
60a	**NCBI** – charity shop; Tony Tang – hairdresser and photographer; Orient – souvenirs; Molloys – sweets; Shudall's – sweets; dwelling house.
62	**Heffernan's** – pub; Hays Castle site.

Houses between the Bullring and Henrietta Street on the seaward side of Main Street often had cellars, or in some cases they appear to have had whole extra floors added below the Main Street level. In this case the top three floors were extended on to Main Street while the lower section complete with fanlight opened on to what would once have been a private wharf or the seashore. (Rossiter Collection)

65	**Dream Drapes** – curtains; Lowney's 147 – snooker club; The Long Rooms – pub; Wickham's – brewery; Harpur & Wickham – brewery.
64	**Colman Doyle** – hardware; Mrs Doyle – grocery; Stephen Doyle.
67	**Shoe Rack** – shoes; Masterpiece – framing; Crowley – paints; Cadogan – electrical and bikes (1962); Underwood – wallpaper and paint.
66/68	**Birkenstock** – shoes; Colman Doyle – paints, etc.; Kevin Roche – fish and chips, and shoe repairs; Sinnott's – bacon shop; James Hayes – boot and shoe warehouse, 'a customer once – a customer always' (1912).
69	**Dun Mhuire** – theatre; Labour Exchange; Garda Barracks; RIC barracks; Devereux townhouse
70	**Lotus House** – restaurant.
71	**Paddy Power** – bookmakers; phone shop; Pettit's – supermarket; Lacey – shoe repairs; Doyle – saddler; Pettit – grocer.
73	**Paddy Power** – bookmakers; Savoy Bar; Osborne's – pubs; David J. Browne – tea, wines and spirits (1914).
75	**Good Fellas** – barbers; Pettit's – supermarket.
72/74	**Gold Rush** – amusements; Finnegan's – pub; Viking – pub; Goal Bar – pub Martin Cahill (1876).
72	**South Main Street** – manure.
76	**Richie Doyle** – butcher.
77	**Ger Hore** – photography; Denis O'Connor – photography; Malones – fish (demolished); Oyster Tavern.
78	**Sublime** – café; Star – café.
79	**Doyle's** – bookmakers; AM PM – general store; Travers-Purcell – pub; Syl Stamp – grocery and spirits; Wexford Supply Stores – grocery, wine and spirits (1888).
80	**Cistin Eile** – restaurant; Into the Blue – restaurant; Kelly's Deli; Kelly – hairdresser; Flynn – chemist.
81	**Pub Take Away**; Xtravision – videos; Wexford Clay Pipe Factory.
82	**Lloyds** – hairdressers; Scissors Empire – hairdresser; O'Connor – pub; Kelly – grocer (1914); Roche – pub.
83	**Bugler Doyle's** – pub; Menapia Bar; Cardiff – tea and spirits.
84	**Subway** – fast food; Dave Allen – cycles (1995); Jeven's – jeweller, 'Mounters, setters of diamonds and precious stones' (1962); Shanahan & Quirke – pawnbrokers (1858).
85/95	Site of Stafford Castle
85	**Star Box** – TV accessory; art shop; Cleary – auctioneer; Billington – leather merchants; Billington – clog factory,
86	**Wexford Insurances**; Allen – cycles; Harvey – meat shop; Radford

	– meat shop; Godkins (Suttons) 'River Plate South American meat', 'open until 4 p.m. Sunday for milk'.
87	**Mojo's** – café (closed); Wexford Insurances; Slevin's – electrical (1962); Murphy – fruit.
88/90	**Brash** - Hairdressers; Aidan Kelly – butchers (1962) public toilets.
89	**Keane's** (closed) – butchers; Morgan – pub; Edward Wickham coxswain of Rosslare Fort lifeboat lived over this after The Fort was washed away in 1925 (lifeboat moored off Ballast Bank).
91	**O'Leary** – travel agent; Singer sewing machines; Kirwan – barber.
92	**Betting shop**; Southside – dry cleaners; Quigley – electrical; James Murphy – tea and spirits, 'We keep only the best teas, wines and spirits and leave our customers to be the judge' (1909).
93	David Condron – provision store (1881).
94	**Murphy** – shoes; Aidan Kelly – butcher.
95/97	**Boyle Sports** – bookmakers; Nicholas Broader's – pub; Hutchinson – pub; Ryan – grocery and spirits (1909).
96	**Colman Doyle** – pet shop; Denis O'Connor – photography (1960); Murphy dwelling house; John North – barber.
98/100	**Colman Doyle** – furniture; red brick house (Tontine Society here).
99	**Wexford Framing** – photography and framing; Codd's – bookmakers; Cullimores – bookmakers.
102	**Crowning Glory** – hairdresser; McGrail's – drapery.
104	**Premier** – chipper; Kelly – dairy.
106	**Donna Marina** – restaurant; Gusto – café; Randall – music; Walsh – greengrocers.
108	**Hayes** – cycles and fishing; Hayes & Kavanagh's – cycles 'late of Pierce's Cycle Factory, practical repairers, enamellers, motor car for hire' (1914); S. Sinnott – jeweller 'Chronometers, repeaters and all kinds of complicated watches have my very careful attention – clocks wound by contract – Spectacles and folders to suit all sights – Special attention given to execution of oculist's prescriptions' (1909).
109	Vacant – Menapia Classic Moulding; Cadogan – bookmaker; Hanton – wallpaper.
98★	**MABS** – Money Advice; Fancy dress shop; Corcoran's – bookmakers; Menapia Classic Moulding; Cadogan – bookmaker; Hanton – wallpaper.
110	**Wexford Auto Factors**; Morgan – newsagent; Cullimores – pub; John Cash – Uillean piper/horse dealer.
100★	**Stable Diet** – café; Mange 2 – restaurant; Indian restaurant; Hannon – grocery; Stafford – provisions.

This door once gave access to the living quarters of what later became Heaton's Department Store. It has since been converted to a small display window. (Rossiter Collection)

112   **Sky & Ground** – pub; Kingdom Bar; Cullimore – pubs.

112a   **Next Door** – off licence; O'Rourke – butcher.

114   **Foggy Dew Inn** – pub; Kingdom – pub; Ridge House – pub; Barnwell's – pub (1960s).

115   **O'Toole's** – sweets, cigarettes, café; O'Toole's – café; Rattigan – jeweller.

116   **Flanagan's** – store; Flower shop; Top Drawer – baby wear; Richard Doyle – bakery, 'Doyle bakes the bread that makes the men' (1909).

117   **Emerald Gardens** – restaurant; Capitol Bar; O'Rourke – pub; Stafford's – pub.

118   **Flanagan's** – amusements; The Club – videos; Granada – amusements; Granada Grill – café (bingo upstairs in aid of Loch Garman Band); Eugene McGrail's – drapery.

119   **Glamour** – hairdressers; O'Neill's – sweets and newsagents; Roche – newsagents; Murphy – newsagents.

120   **Colman Doyle** – furniture; Capitol Cinema; Stafford – furniture; Unknown – barrel factory.

121   **O'Leary** – auctioneer; Bargains Galore – drapery; Patrick Kelly – provisions.

122   **Colman Doyle** – furniture; Bank of Ireland finance; dwelling house (engineer on Wexford Bridge 1959 lived here).